I HOPE
THIS EMAIL
FINDS YOU
NEVER

KEN KUPCHIK

ILLUSTRATED BY EMILY ANN HILL

I HOPE THIS EMAIL FINDS YOU NEVER

The Official Guide to Blissfully Surviving the Modern Workplace

HarperCollins
LEADERSHIP

AN IMPRINT OF HarperCollins

Published by HarperCollins Leadership,
an imprint of HarperCollins Focus LLC.

Any internet addresses, phone numbers, or company or product information printed in this book are offered as a resource and are not intended in any way to be or to imply an endorsement by HarperCollins Leadership, nor does HarperCollins Leadership vouch for the existence, content, or services of these sites, phone numbers, companies, or products beyond the life of this book.

Book design by Aubrey Khan, Neuwirth & Associates, Inc.

ISBN 978-1-4002-3282-6 (eBook)
ISBN 978-1-4002-3281-9 (TP)

Library of Congress Control Number: 2022940855

Printed in the United States of America
22 23 24 25 26 LSC 10 9 8 7 6 5 4 3 2 1

CONTENTS

PART 3

Coworkers

(Getting Along with Your Fellow Inmates)

PART 4

Working Remotely

(Wink, Wink)

PART 5

Meetings
(Whose Foot Is That?)

PART 6

Surviving the Day-to-Day
(Lord, Give Me the Strength)

PART 7

Termination of Employment
(Let's Pretend We Liked Each Other)

GETTING STARTED

Congratulations, you've been hired at ~~your dream~~ a job. Given how competitive it is in today's world, that's quite an accomplishment. It takes countless hours to search through job postings, go through multiple rounds of video interviews, and to click that "I'm not a robot" thing on the employer's website. And after all that, you still have to find out where the hiring manager lives so you can drop off a cash bribe at her house. Exhausting!

Now that you've put that stress behind you, it's time to move onto new stress. Luckily, you won't have to wait long, because there's nothing quite as nerve-racking as the modern workplace.

Unlike most workplace books, however, this one won't sugarcoat, deflect, or mislead. We won't bore you with some business

titan's life story, and we won't try to convince you that if you just follow a trendy new self-improvement fad, you'll be promoted to CEO.

So what *will* we do?

Well, look, uh—we're on a deadline here, so can you stop asking so many questions and just read on?

Thanks.

PART 1

Employee Orientation
(The Descent)

Starting a new job can be overwhelming. There are people to meet, information to digest, and lots of preparation required to counter the lies you told on your résumé. Whether you're an experienced employee or new to the workforce, you can be sure that at some point in your first few days, you'll start to wonder whether you've made a grave mistake (you have).

The good news is that your new employer has invested time and resources into a comprehensive indoctrination process known as "new-hire orientation." It's during this process when you'll be introduced to your coworkers, sign paperwork allowing the company to compensate you the bare minimum possible, and get an early glimpse at which flavor of dysfunction plagues your new workplace.

But don't sweat the small stuff. Sweat the big stuff instead, because you'll have plenty to worry about once you get through orientation. But for now, it's best to sit back and let the company believe they can mold you into the perfect employee. Little do they know that's a battle they've already lost.

Making Awkward Introductions Better (or Exponentially Worse)

There's nothing quite like meeting your coworkers for the first time. Or maybe there is—we actually don't really know. In any case, whether they're done in person or remotely, introductions can be fun because you have a chance to present the best fake version of yourself that your coworkers will ever see.

But it's important to be cautious when making introductions. If done correctly, a good first impression can help you build rapport and ingratiate you to your new coworkers. A bad first impression, however, can ruin a relationship right away, before you get a chance to ruin it gradually, over a longer period of time. So put on your best fake smile and pretend to be somebody that you're not—it's likely to pay off.

SOME TIPS TO HELP YOU IMPRESS YOUR NEW COWORKERS

Tip #1: Dress professionally
The way you present yourself is important, which is why you should always dress professionally when starting a new role. Even if your company doesn't have a strict dress code, make sure to pick

a nice outfit to wear on your first few days. It's important to deceive the people you'll be working with, so don't discount your appearance. After all, everyone knows that it's what's on the outside that *really* matters.

Tip #2: Remember people's names

If you want to impress your new coworkers, make it a point to remember their names. Not only will this show that you were paying attention, it will also make them feel important. You can do this by repeating their name over and over again as loud as possible while they're talking, or by taking a photo and adding the name to it with a caption. They'll be more than appreciative.

Tip #3: Be an active listener

Most people want to be heard, and in today's fast-paced world, those who are able to listen can build lasting and more meaningful relationships. When meeting your new coworkers, try to be an active listener by letting them speak, asking open-ended questions, and nodding along as they bore you to tears. If you want to go a step further, take notes after the conversation is over, then leave the notes on your coworkers' desks to prove you were listening to what they said.

SOME ADDITIONAL TIPS

1. Smile and make eye contact. Try to hold it for a few seconds. Now look away from the mirror. It'll be even harder with a real person.
2. Make a self-deprecating joke to show everyone you're mentally prepared to be deprecated by them too.
3. Ask your coworkers questions to spark conversation. Try to keep it professional. A good rule of thumb is to never ask the questions you *really* want to ask.

4. Send a follow-up email to the people you've met. Keep it friendly and concise. *Do not* sign the email with "Love," or "Yours truly."

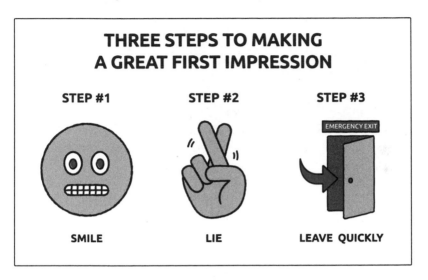

THREE STEPS TO MAKING A GREAT FIRST IMPRESSION

STEP #1   **STEP #2**   **STEP #3**

EMERGENCY EXIT

SMILE   **LIE**   **LEAVE QUICKLY**

WHAT NOT TO DO

1. Don't share too much information about yourself. This can backfire the same way it's backfired in every single one of your relationships.
2. Similarly, try to stay away from personal questions such as whether they have a therapist they could recommend.
3. Don't interrupt somebody who is introducing themselves to you, even if you're excited about finally meeting a Cornelius in real life.
4. Don't be overly complimentary. You might need to bad-mouth this person to your coworkers later on.
5. If you've forgotten someone's name, don't try to guess. Instead, just mumble something unintelligible under your breath and hope they don't call you out.

FINAL THOUGHTS

Your goal during introductions shouldn't be to impress everyone, since doing so would mean setting yourself up to do more work. Instead, you should strive to convince your new coworkers that you're professional, conscientious, and approachable—that is, the opposite of who you really are.

But introductions are merely the first of many interactions you'll have with your coworkers, so while they're certainly a great way to start things off, they're not the end-all, be-all. So if you've somehow managed to screw up your introduction, don't worry— all you've done is given yourself a head start.

Sign Without Reading: Filling Out Your New-Hire Paperwork

Because we have "laws," and because companies don't want to be "sued" into "bankruptcy," when you start a new job, you'll be required to fill out lots of boring paperwork. This paperwork is usually mandated by the government, or has been prepared by the company's lawyers to ensure they can take ownership of your organs if you happen to die while in the office.

Since most people can't afford a lawyer to review these documents, we've put together a quick explainer of your new-hire checklist. (Warning: if your employer doesn't provide paperwork, you've probably been roped into a pyramid scheme by that guy you haven't seen since high school.) Please note that the following is strictly for entertainment purposes and should not be construed as legal advice—neither one of us was smart enough to get into law school.

EMPLOYMENT CONTRACT

This document will usually lay out the terms of your employment—things like your work schedule, compensation, employee responsibilities, and termination conditions.

Tip: Using a pen to add another 0 onto your salary probably won't work.

FORMS REQUIRED BY LAW

The government makes you fill out this paperwork since they know you won't send them money on a pinky promise. This usually includes a W-4, an I-9, and possibly a WW3, a 666, and a WAP.

Tip: If you don't feel like filling out these forms, just send the government a letter saying, "I don't think so," and you'll be exempt.

INTERNAL FORMS

Despite their name, these forms have nothing to do with what's inside your body. Internal forms concern your relationship with the company and include noncompete and nondisclosure agreements, employee handbook documents, and drug- and/or alcohol-test consent agreements.

Tip: If you're asked to sign a drug-test consent agreement, it's a bad idea to violently rip it to pieces in front of the hiring manager.

BENEFITS DOCUMENTS

Some benefits are required by law, and some are offered to employees to lure them away from even more sociopathic employers. Common benefits include health and life insurance, paid time off, sick leave, retirement plans, and disability insurance. Unfortunately, really hating your job is not a disability.

Tip: Make sure to max out your 401(k) contribution so that you have even less money to enjoy your life right now.

NONDISCLOSURE AGREEMENTS

A nondisclosure agreement is a contract between at least two parties that outlines confidential material, knowledge, or information that the parties wish to share but wish to restrict access to. This is just a fancy way of saying that you can't repeat some of the things you've learned when you work at a company.

Tip: You can avoid being liable for your eventual betrayal by simply signing someone else's name—this will easily stand up in court.

KEEPING COPIES FOR YOUR RECORDS

While you might be comfortable entrusting your fate to a multinational conglomerate, it's still recommended that you make and keep copies of all your new-hire documents. In the event of a termination or a lawsuit, they might come in handy, though you'll want to be sure the document outlining your salary is hidden away if you have any hope of ever keeping a boyfriend or girlfriend.

Tip: When altering documents in order to help you win your legal case, watch for typos and smudged ink, which are obvious signs of tampering.

FINAL THOUGHTS

The legal documents you're forced to sign after starting a new job might look intimidating, but in reality, they're a lot worse than that. Depending on what you sign, you might be giving up your privacy, your legal recourse, and even your future earnings, which would make the owner of the sub shop next door to your apartment extremely unhappy.

This is why you should always pretend that you've read your new-hire paperwork carefully before signing it. And if there's anything you don't understand, don't worry about it, because there's no way you're going to quit after going through all that trouble to get hired in the first place. So go ahead and sign your future away—at least you'll still have your past.

Better Than Ambien: Employee Training

Your training period is when the company ~~tries to brainwash you~~ formally starts the education process. It's a great time to soak up knowledge, better understand workplace dynamics, and scroll through Instagram so you can see all the people who are having fun because their parents are rich.

Training, which can be done virtually or in person, will usually be led by a specialized trainer, a human resources director, or your new supervisor, although some employers will put you in a room with a TV as if you're a child. In any event, it's important to take notes and pay attention, especially when people are discussing what to order for lunch.

WHAT IS EMPLOYEE TRAINING?

Employee training provides new hires with the requisite skills and knowledge required to carry out the functions of their job. Whether the skills being taught are broad or specific to a particular role, they will be presented in the most boring, depressing, and unpleasant way possible. And, unless you're one of the lucky few who have retained their ability to focus in the face of smartphone-induced aimlessness, it's very likely that you will leave employee training with less confidence about your knowledge and abilities than when you arrived.

THE TYPES OF EMPLOYEE TRAINING

Companies use different training methods to educate their staff. Here are the most common:

- **Classroom training:** This method, designed to invoke memories of the crippling anxiety you felt in high school, is one of the most effective types of employee training and is typically used by big organizations to quickly crush dissent.
- **One-on-one training:** While more personalized, this type of training isn't for everyone and makes it nearly impossible to spend your training period screwing around. During one-on-one training, a manager or an experienced employee is instructed to follow you everywhere you go, including the restroom.
- **Online training:** This is usually the most time-intensive type of training, though it has its upsides. Whether it's an online course, or a few days of video training, online education allows you to do whatever you want, as long as you occasionally toggle your cursor so the computer screen doesn't lock you out.

TIPS TO GET THE MOST OUT OF YOUR TRAINING

- If the training is in person, try to sit in the middle of the room. If you sit too close to the front, your coworkers will think you're a suck-up. And if you sit too far back, you'll get the last pick of any snacks that get passed around.
- It can be useful to jot down anything that might help you perform your duties. You don't have to make notes for everything, but definitely write down that you have to show up every day, even on Thursday and Friday.

- Occasionally asking questions can show that you're engaged, and nodding along every now and then will make it seem like you're not daydreaming about marrying a frail, wealthy person who is near death, just to put an end to this charade.
- Feel free to discuss what you've learned with your fellow new hires offline, but remember that one of them is very likely to become your archenemy in the not-so-distant future.

THINGS EMPLOYEE TRAINING SHOULD PROBABLY COVER BUT DOES NOT

- which excuses are most compelling/believable when asking for time off
- how to identify which coworker is most likely to guilt you into donating to their GoFundMe campaign
- the absolute bare minimum output required to maintain employment
- the location of the best hiding spots in the office where you can go to cry
- which company executive is most susceptible to entrapment and subsequent blackmail
- on precisely which days the company plans to administer drug and/or alcohol screenings
- which ruthless social climber is most likely to throw you under the bus

THINGS YOU COULD BE DOING IF YOU WEREN'T STUCK IN TRAINING

- learning a new language
- applying to grad school
- spying on your neighbors
- making a collage of all your job-rejection emails
- monetizing your pet turtle Bartholomew's Instagram account
- trying to binge the entire Netflix catalog
- joining a cult
- gaining twenty pounds

FINAL THOUGHTS

Employee training is a great opportunity to learn about your new workplace and to get to know some of the people you'll be working with. If you find any of it dull and boring, don't worry, the job itself will be dull and boring too.

So try to make the most of your training period, whether it lasts a few days or stretches into weeks or months. This will be your best opportunity to relax before you're thrown into the rigor of highly demanding labor. And if you can learn something while you're at it, great! But if not, that's okay too—don't be so hard on yourself. After all, *they* hired *you*. If anything, they're the ones who are at fault.

Corporatespeak: Why Upper Managers Talk Like Cult Leaders

I f you've ever sat through a corporate seminar or scrolled through LinkedIn, you've probably noticed some of the language used by executives and business influencers sounds conspicuously like the language used by cult leaders.

There's a reason for this.

Business leaders are responsible for motivating their employees, and in exchange, they get dump trucks full of money delivered to their palatial estates. It's a totally fair exchange, and you should definitely never question it, ever. Instead, just repeat corporate buzzwords to your coworkers until they can no longer question your loyalty.

COMMON PHRASES

Here are some phrases commonly used by business leaders followed by what they *really* mean:

Phrase: "We're all in this together."
What it really means: You're definitely on your own here.
Phrase: "We care about your safety."
What it really means: There's no way we'd be doing this if it wasn't legally mandated.

Phrase: "We believe in work-life balance."
What it really means: Get used to working nights and weekends until you die.
Phrase: "This is a great opportunity."
What it really means: We can't find anybody else who's willing to do this.
Phrase: "We're going to pivot."
What it really means: Within weeks, you will be unemployed.
Phrase: "We need to embrace risk."
What it really means: I will soon be in prison for corporate fraud.
Phrase: "Keep me in the loop."
What it really means: Do not, under any circumstances, keep me in the loop.
Phrase: "We need to think outside the box."
What it really means: My father got me this job.
Phrase: "This wasn't an easy decision."
What it really means: This was literally the easiest decision we've ever made.
Phrase: "There's a lot of synergy on this."
What it really means: My wife and I are hurtling toward divorce.

ACRONYMS

Oftentimes, people in the workplace will use acronyms when communicating. Here are some common acronyms you might come across and what they mean:

EOD: End of day
OOO: Out of office
WFH: Work from home
WFRB: Work from Russian bathhouse
NSFW: Not safe for work
NSFK: Not safe for kittens

TY: Thank you
FU: Finally understanding
PAIN: Please answer, I'm nervous
INH: I need ham
LIE: Legally, I'm exonerated

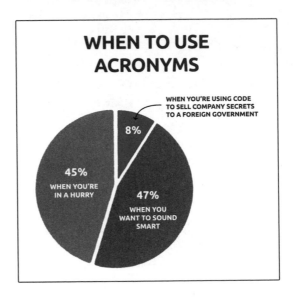

BUZZWORDS

The following corporate buzzwords really don't mean anything, but using them frequently can help keep you on track for a promotion. Here are some examples used in a sentence:

Ecosystem: It's unfortunate that our company is rapidly destroying the planet's *ecosystem*, but we need the money.

Disruptive: Can someone please ask Rachel to stop blasting Ace of Base at her desk? It's very *disruptive.*

Open the kimono: This one is just weird.

Push the envelope: During the meeting, *push the envelope* full of cash toward the federal regulator so he knows it's for him.

Bandwidth: For the company holiday party, let's find a *bandwidth* a keyboard player.

Scalable: Do you think the wall outside the office is *scalable*? I can't take it here anymore.

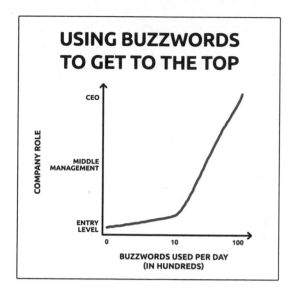

FINAL THOUGHTS

While it might feel a bit strange to be surrounded by people who sound like they've been lobotomized, rest assured: the only reason they talk like that is because they'll do anything for money. So if you're ever in doubt about what to say, simply repeat a few buzzwords—they don't even have to be in any coherent order—and your coworkers will practically trip over themselves agreeing with you.

But if you find yourself unwilling to go along with the crowd and decide that the entire premise of talking in corporate jargon is absurd, be aware of the risks of going against the crowd. As far as the company is concerned, you're not there to show your individualism, to have opinions, or to be a sentient being. You're there to obey. So make your choice, but choose wisely—your meager paycheck depends on it.

How Long You Can Get Away with Being "New" Until You're Held Accountable

In addition to the excitement afforded by finally being able to pay your bills, starting a new job can also give you quite a bit of leeway when it comes to accountability. Most employers don't expect new hires to perform their jobs perfectly from day one, which provides an opportunity for you to take a minivacation of sorts right after you start.

But be careful: if you overplay your hand, you might draw too much attention to yourself. And if there's one thing you always want to avoid at work, it's being seen.

THINGS YOU CAN GET AWAY WITH WHEN YOU'RE NEW

- showing up late because you got lost
- wearing something that violates the company's dress code
- mispronouncing your coworker's name (only once)
- drinking a coworker's Honest Tea (only once)
- parking in a reserved spot (unless it belongs to your manager or the CEO)
- spilling your coffee all over the kitchen floor (surprisingly, you can do this every day)

- missing a Zoom meeting due to "technical issues"
- putting a picture of an anteater in your email signature

While the honeymoon period can be great, remember that your early days with a company can set the tone for the rest of your tenure. Don't push the envelope and risk burning through your goodwill right away. Instead, burn through your goodwill slowly, making sure it lasts over the duration of your time there.

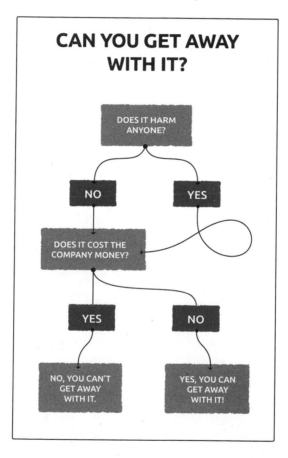

THINGS YOU CAN'T GET AWAY WITH EVEN IF YOU'RE NEW

- crossing out a coworker's name on their lunch bag and writing in your own
- locking yourself inside a coworker's office and refusing to leave
- asking everyone to refer to you as "the future CEO"
- refusing to do your assigned tasks because the "vibes are off"
- purposely locking yourself out of your computer in an effort to avoid having to do any work
- setting an automated away message titled "nap time" between noon and 3:30 p.m.
- asking your coworkers to write testimonials for your online dating profile

HOW TO TELL THAT YOU'RE NO LONGER CONSIDERED NEW

Before you know it, you'll no longer be seen as the "new" hire. Here are some signs of when that happens:

- Everyone remembers your name.
- You've developed a circle of coworkers you're friendly with, all of whom will eventually abandon you.
- People become visibly angry at you when you make a mistake.
- The emails you receive from management are less passive-aggressive and more active-aggressive.
- You're asked to train a new coworker (who will eventually replace you).
- People reprimand you for spilling coffee on the kitchen floor.

Once you've reached this stage, it's time to dial it back. A company's patience can only extend so far without the threat of a lawsuit. This doesn't mean you can't get away with a lot (more on that later), it just means that it's time to buckle down and learn how to make it look like you're working hard.

FINAL THOUGHTS

Whether you're the type of person who likes to hit the ground running, or the type that likes to ease into a role, the first few months at a new job should be happy months. After all, you're making money, getting lots of leeway, and haven't had a chance to see anyone's true colors (or to reveal your own) just yet.

But it's also important to keep an eye on the big picture. You're likely to stay in your new workplace until you either win big on a scratch ticket (unlikely) or find a job that aligns with your passions (extremely unlikely). So make sure to settle in for the long haul. Once you're with an employer, they're likely to keep you around for a while, unless they can save a few cents, in which case, they'll get rid of you immediately.

The Bright Side: Getting Paid

While this book might (accurately) portray the modern-day workplace as a stress-inducing cringe factory run by merciless tyrants determined to extract every ounce of productivity from their workers at the expense of their physical and emotional well-being, there is a bright side: money!

Not only can money make up for some of the more complicated emotions that tend to bubble up as a result of workplace stress, it can also help provide seed funding for an elaborate financial scam that will finally allow you to be your own boss—a win-win.

But before you get too excited about your take-home pay, you should remember that money isn't everything, it's just the only thing standing between you and pure, unadulterated happiness, a bliss unknown to anyone except the lucky few who bathe in fountains of freedom and pleasure while the rest of us toil away at our computers, surrounded by drab, beige-colored walls.

IMPORTANT FACTS ABOUT PAYCHECKS

- Most workers get paychecks through direct deposit.
- Most employees get paychecks weekly or every two weeks.
- Paychecks are never big enough.
- The withholdings from your paycheck can be difficult to understand, so don't bother trying.
- The time in between paychecks is too long.

- Getting two paychecks at once would be kind of awesome.

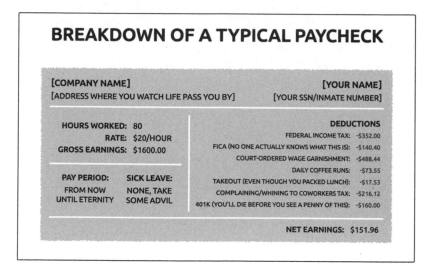

DISCUSSING MONEY AT WORK

While there has long been an unspoken social rule that says you shouldn't discuss money with your coworkers, your employer can't legally prevent you from discussing your salary, and many labor activists and progressive employers actively encourage it, at least partially because they're being nosy.

Pros of discussing money
- more leverage when negotiating pay
- helps level the playing field among employees
- getting to brag
- helps identify which coworkers to ask if you need to borrow money

Cons of discussing money
- Somebody's feelings might get hurt.
- That somebody will probably be you.

Money can be a fraught subject in the workplace, so it's important to handle the topic in a mature and professional manner, unless you feel you've been wronged, in which case a full-on meltdown might be the way to go. But always remember: you can catch more flies with honey than with vinegar—a phrase, we should note, that was coined before we knew that bees were dying at an alarming rate, raising questions about the future supply of honey. (Meanwhile, there appears to be no similar shortage of vinegar.)

HOW TO HANDLE PROBLEMS WITH YOUR PAYCHECK

- Gather the necessary documents and records.
- Review the pay issues you want to discuss with your supervisor or manager, who might refer you to human resources.
- Try to discuss the issues in a calm and rational manner while clenching your fists and gritting your teeth.
- Refrain from threatening to file a formal complaint and instead make it a promise.
- Make sure to keep a copy of all correspondence for your records and for the FBI.

Once you've started receiving a regular paycheck, it's a good idea to plan ahead. Budgeting for the future can help put you on sound financial footing and ensure you have enough money saved to weather a rainy day. With that being said, spending all your money on food and designer clothes is actually way more fun and feels way better.

FINANCIAL PLANNING TIPS

- Try to pay off debt.
- Build up an emergency fund with six months' worth of living expenses.

- Contribute a portion of your income to a retirement plan such as a 401(k) or an IRA.
- Always make regularly scheduled payments toward Mafia loans.
- Buy four thousand copies of this book.
- Allocate at least 20 percent of your income to cheese.
- Do not, under any circumstances, let your uncle Frank borrow money.

HEALTH INSURANCE AND OTHER BENEFITS

In addition to your pay, many employers are forced by the government to generously offer health insurance and other benefits as part of your compensation package.

These benefits can vary widely from employer to employer, though most workplaces will at a minimum cover the cost of removing your body from the building in the event that you die in the middle of the workday.

COMMON TYPES OF EMPLOYEE BENEFITS

- health, dental, vision, and life insurance
- paid time off such as sick days and vacation days
- retirement benefits or accounts
- permission to use the bathroom sometimes
- free paper towels to wipe away tears
- a terse Happy Birthday email once a year
- a stained, barely functioning Keurig that grudgingly spouts brown coffee-flavored water

STOCK OPTIONS

In some cases, an employer may offer stock options as part of your compensation package. Stock options are a vehicle that gives someone the right to buy or sell shares of a particular stock at a specified price. If all of that sounds confusing, it's because you, like us, are not and will never be rich.

Here's how stock options *really* work:

1. An employer will offer a stock grant, which will list a grant date as well as how many shares the employee may eventually own.
2. The employee will become excited, knowing they own a piece of the company and have an opportunity to strike it rich.
3. After doing the math, the employee will realize they've been granted the equivalent of a one-week gift card to Chipotle.

FINAL THOUGHTS

Having a steady source of income can give people stability, a sense of pride, and a higher limit on their credit card. It's also the reason why most of us are willing to wake up every day and stumble into our morning meetings, wary, red-eyed, and desperate for caffeine.

But, as you'll see further into this book, money alone usually isn't enough to keep employees engaged, unless it's a ton of money, in which case it probably is. A sense of community, belonging, and a commitment to a shared mission is what will truly drive you to become your best self, so you should look for a place that offers these things on nights and weekends, because you definitely won't find them at work.

PART 2

General Workplace Etiquette

(No Eye Contact before 11:00 a.m.)

Once you've settled into your new routine and milked being new for all it's worth, you'll want to adopt the unwritten rules of the workplace. Oftentimes, these rules will be observable without actually being documented, not unlike the rules of a prison gang.

While it might be tempting to ignore them, it would be a mistake to assume these rules don't matter. Following general workplace etiquette can strengthen your relationship with coworkers and solidify your position within the company, while going against it can alienate your fellow employees and draw unwanted attention, though in some ways, all attention at work could be considered unwanted.

What follows is an attempt to document and clarify the unspoken rules of the workplace and to give you a road map that will help you blend in. Keep in mind that some workplaces will have their own unspoken rules, so pay attention to what your coworkers are doing, but do it subtly, without staring, and without following anyone out to their car.

Manners, Greetings, Salutations, and Conversations Preapproved by HR

Having good manners can help you excel in the workplace, unless you want to become a senior manager or an executive, in which case the exact opposite is true. Regardless, our daily encounters with coworkers offer opportunities to put our best foot forward and to strengthen workplace bonds.

A good rule of thumb is to treat others the way you want to be treated, though it's unlikely anyone will be willing to give you a deep-tissue massage while feeding you Ferrero Rochers. But no matter whom you're addressing, whether it's the janitor or the CEO, you should always lead with respect, especially if it's the janitor, who is likely to be a key witness in your eventual slip-and-fall personal injury lawsuit.

TEN RULES FOR WORKPLACE MANNERS

1. Say please and thank you.
2. Don't interrupt.
3. Don't try to force your coworkers to watch all five seasons of *Breaking Bad.*
4. Don't give unsolicited advice.

5. Don't refer to the elevator as the "magic gravity box."
6. Don't make personal remarks about someone's appearance or clothing.
7. Don't accuse someone of committing the Isabella Stewart Gardner art heist.
8. Don't pry open your coworker's locked desk drawer in a desperate attempt to steal their snacks.
9. Clean up after yourself.
10. When passing someone in the hall, always do that weird tight-lipped smile thing.

WHAT TO SAY (AND WHAT NOT TO SAY)

In the workplace, *what* you say is just as important as *how* you say it, so choosing your words carefully should always be top of mind. Here are some examples of common language you might use in the workplace, contrasted with some less professional alternatives:

Acceptable: "Thanks for taking the time to go over this."
Not Acceptable: "I appreciate you graciously setting aside a few precious minutes for me, Your Highness."
Acceptable: "Would you mind clarifying that a bit?"
Not Acceptable: "The ol' brain's not working so hot today, eh?"
Acceptable: "Do you need any help on this?"
Not Acceptable: "I will literally pay you to stop emailing me."
Acceptable: "I understand where you're coming from."
Not Acceptable: "Our selfish society has warped my capacity for empathy, so I'm incapable, and unwilling, to see anyone's perspective except my own."

COMMON WORKPLACE ETIQUETTE MISTAKES

The following are some frequent workplace etiquette mistakes you'll want to avoid:

- being late to meetings or appointments
- checking your phone in the middle of a conversation
- having a conversation in the middle of checking your phone
- hiring a contractor to remodel the break room without asking for permission
- interrupting your boss while she is in the middle of firing you
- trying to make small talk with somebody who is busy insider trading the company's stock
- not covering your mouth when you cough or sneeze during an office fire

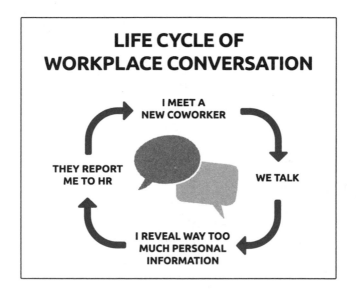

LIFE CYCLE OF WORKPLACE CONVERSATION

I MEET A NEW COWORKER

WE TALK

I REVEAL WAY TOO MUCH PERSONAL INFORMATION

THEY REPORT ME TO HR

GREETINGS

The way we greet people at work might seem trivial, but it's important to treat coworkers with respect and to be mindful of how and when you address them. In many cases, we spend more time with the people we work with than with our families, but this does *not* give you the right to scream, "I wish you were never born" in their face before running upstairs and slamming the door.

Rules for greeting coworkers
- Make eye contact (after 11:00 a.m.).
- Say "Hello," "Hi," or "Good morning."
- Address people by their chosen name unless it's really long; then just avoid them altogether.
- If you can't remember someone's name, either politely ask them to tell you or just call them by the name of the lead character in the last TV show you watched.
- Never greet your workplace nemesis.

EMAIL AND MESSAGING ETIQUETTE

With the rise of remote work, email and interoffice messaging platforms have become the primary mode of communication for millions of workers. While helpful, these mediums have their own unspoken rules of what is and isn't acceptable. Here are some rules to remember:

Email etiquette
- Include a clear, direct subject line.
- Avoid using "reply all" unless absolutely necessary.
- Make sure to set up a signature block with your name, title, and all passwords to your personal accounts clearly listed.
- Always use as many exclamation points as possible.
- Be cautious with humor—you've been joking around your whole life and look where it got you.
- Avoid shrinking the font size down to the smallest possible option so that it's more difficult to read your message.
- Before sending, double-check to make sure you've selected the correct recipient—there's no need to bore anyone else with your pointless diatribes.

Messaging etiquette
- You should know the person you're messaging.
- Start with a short greeting.
- Once they've responded, send them the "squid" emoji to throw them off their game.
- Try to respond with "lol" after every message.
- Never send bad news via instant message.
- If somebody is taking a long time to respond, send a question mark every five seconds until you get an answer.

CONVERSATION STARTERS

Starting conversations with your coworkers can help strengthen workplace relationships, so when you eventually move on, people will remember you for ten minutes instead of five. Here are some conversation starters you can use to get people talking:

- Did you have a nice weekend?
- Are there any books or podcasts that you would recommend?
- Have you ever stared into the abyss?
- Do you listen to any cool local bands?
- Do you have any fun hobbies? I like to water the plastic plants in the front lobby.
- Do you know why my father abandoned me?
- Does this chicken smell bad to you?

TOPICS OF CONVERSATION

Humans are inherently social creatures, which is why we're naturally drawn to conversations with our coworkers. In today's workplace, however, it's important to understand what is and isn't acceptable in everyday discussions. For instance, calling somebody a "social creature" has the potential to be misconstrued, so try not to do that.

Topics to avoid
- politics
- controversial current events
- religion
- the fact that Alf ate cats
- the details of your CEO's elaborate Ponzi scheme
- the fact that you're the one who broke the ice maker in the break room
- your sex life (other people's sex lives are okay to discuss)
- why you carry a signed, prewritten letter of resignation folded in your pocket at all times

Appropriate topics
- anything work-related
- the weather
- sports
- your justifications for eating an entire pizza before 11:00 a.m.
- the surveillance van parked outside the office
- investing in your CEO's Ponzi scheme
- travel, specifically to countries without extradition treaties
- forming a union

FINAL THOUGHTS

It might be tempting to behave the same way around your co-workers as you do around your friends, but the difference is that your friends (probably) aren't getting paid to spend time with you. This is why having good manners and following the unspoken rules of workplace etiquette are so important—being around you is already difficult enough.

Looking beyond that, choosing your words carefully can actually help your career. Knowing how to talk and interact with coworkers is a valuable skill set, and many people get promoted simply due to their ability to communicate.

So, if you're going to show up at work every day, you might as well use your best manners. If nothing else, it can help cover for your complete lack of desirable skills.

The Only Two Times You're Allowed to Touch Somebody You Work With

Whether virtually or in person, we spend so much time with our coworkers that it's natural to grow comfortable around each other. Because of this, the boundaries of professionalism can sometimes blur, creating an atmosphere that feels more permissive than it might actually be.

One of the most common ways employees cross the line (sometimes without even knowing it) is through physical touch, even with a simple pat on the shoulder or a friendly hug. It might seem harmless enough, but it could make some people feel uncomfortable, so always err on the side of caution and keep your grubby hands to yourself.

THE FIVE-SECOND RULE?

Some workplace etiquette experts recommend following the five-second rule.[1] This rule states that it's okay to offer a light tap on the shoulder or a quick pat on the back as long as it doesn't last longer than five seconds.

---

1 This rule is not to be confused with the other five-second rule, which refers to eating food off the floor if it's been there for less than five seconds. The food rule remains approved.

The problem with the five-second rule is twofold. First, how do you know when it's been five seconds? Are you going to use a stopwatch or a cell-phone timer? The second (and more important) concern is that some people don't want to be touched *at all*, ever, which is absolutely their right.

So, rather than following an imaginary five-second rule, follow a different rule instead: keep your hands to yourself. It's an easy way to avoid making other people feel physically uncomfortable— leave that to the Mexican food they had for lunch.

THE EXCEPTIONS

While keeping your hands to yourself is always a safe bet, there are two exceptions. These are the only circumstances under which it's okay to touch somebody you work with.

1. Handshakes

The handshake is one of the most common ways to greet people in the workplace. It consists of mashing your clammy, germ-ridden palm against somebody else's in an awkward, disease-spreading ritual that can be traced back to fifth-century Greece. It's also one of the only times you can touch a coworker.

Tips for an effective handshake:

- Make sure your hands are clean and dry. You can air out your hand by blowing on it or waving it around as if it's on fire.
- Show confidence by initiating the handshake. Establish further initiative by letting out a primal scream at the exact moment your palms touch.
- When initiating a handshake, use welcoming body language to show that you've practiced acting like someone who doesn't lock themselves in the house with their cats and half a dozen boxes of Hungry Man meals every weekend.

- Create a firm grip by applying pressure between your palm and thumb, then add additional pressure by asking the person to explain the Pythagorean theorem.
- Maintain eye contact while shaking hands. This will create a more personal connection, which will be eviscerated the second you open your mouth.
- Use appropriate timing. Pump your hand up and down once or twice then release your grip. If the other person tries to pull away, *do not* release. It's not over until you say it's over.

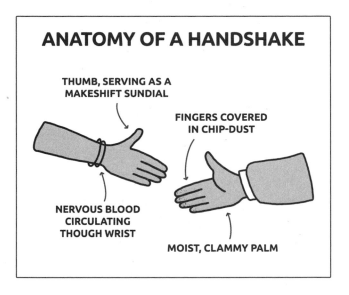

ANATOMY OF A HANDSHAKE

THUMB, SERVING AS A MAKESHIFT SUNDIAL

FINGERS COVERED IN CHIP-DUST

NERVOUS BLOOD CIRCULATING THOUGH WRIST

MOIST, CLAMMY PALM

While a handshake can project confidence and help build rapport, it's not always necessary. Here are some instances when you might want to forego a handshake:

- if you're sick or not feeling well
- if you're uncomfortable shaking hands with the person
- if you've just dipped your hands in crushed glass in preparation for an underground kickboxing match
- if you suffer from chirophobia (a fear of hands)

- if you're using both hands to hold a massive burrito
- if the other person refers to their hand as "the claw"

2. Medical emergencies

The second instance when you're allowed to touch a coworker is when they're having a medical emergency and it's necessary in order to assist them. This includes things like CPR (cardiopulmonary resuscitation), the Heimlich maneuver, or helping to bandage up a wound.

Medical events that might require contact:

- heart attack
- seizure
- treating a burn
- drowning (in a sea of despair)
- helping someone escape a building fire that you deliberately set
- treating a snake bite from one of those two-faced snakes in marketing

Medical events that do not require contact:

- sneeze
- stomachache
- headache brought about by a super annoying email
- hand injury as result of a salesperson punching a hole in the wall
- heart attack faked in order to get out of completing an Excel spreadsheet

HUGGING

Hugging is a gray area. Some workplace experts believe that hugging is fine as long as the power dynamics are equal and the appropriate cues are present. Others believe that touching should be limited to handshakes and that all other contact should be strictly forbidden.

While the pro-hug lobby offered us tens of thousands of dollars to bolster their position, we agree with the uptight scolds and believe the best approach is to play it safe and avoid workplace hugging. This aligns with our general philosophy of doing as little in the workplace as possible.

However, if you do engage in a consensual hug with a willing coworker, here are some ways to make sure it's not misconstrued:

- Try to read the room: cultures can vary by workplace and industry, so make sure hugging is an accepted way to express your attachment disorder.
- Be mindful of power dynamics: avoid hugging with your direct reports or anyone who is junior to you. There's already a high probability that these people would like to stay as far away from you as humanly possible.
- Avoid hugging anyone you might be dating in the workplace as you risk the other people you're dating in the workplace seeing you.
- Don't whisper anything in the other person's ear when hugging them, unless it's the password to a Swiss bank account where the money you've embezzled is being stored.

FINAL THOUGHTS

Even though some innocent workplace touching is permitted, it's best to play it safe and keep your hands where they belong: on your face, wiping the tears that are constantly streaming down your cheeks.

Not only will this ensure that you don't make anyone feel uncomfortable, it will also keep your office interactions professional, making it easier to pass yourself off as a productive and highly engaged employee.

Avoiding Gossip and Drama (Or Embracing It If That's Your Thing)

Once you've joined the professional world, you may believe that the gossip, drama, and popularity contests from your high school days are over, and that you'll be surrounded by professional adults who operate respectfully and always mind their business.

Well, guess again, dummy!

The modern workplace not only contains all the cliques and rumor mills of your average high school. It's even worse because now all the gossips and bullies have money, titles, and coded language that they can use to destroy you professionally if you refuse to bend the knee and indulge their sociopathic tendencies.

All of this makes navigating interoffice drama a critical part of your employment, for better or worse, but definitely mostly for worse.

CAUSES OF WORKPLACE DRAMA

Much like the debilitating anxiety you feel every Sunday night, workplace drama seems to spring out of nowhere. In reality, a well-functioning workplace should have as little drama as possible, which means that most office drama has a cause, like one of the following:

- a negative workplace culture
- a lack of clearly defined rules and standards
- the fact that you work for a company that produces telenovelas
- a curse from a witch or warlock
- the coworker who wears a shirt that says *#drama* on it
- you

HOW TO AVOID OFFICE DRAMA

While it's unlikely that you can avoid workplace drama in its entirety, the following are some rules you can follow to keep your nose clean and your life drama free:

Rule #1: Stick to the facts

When having discussions with your coworkers, keep the conversation focused on facts and stay away from discussing anybody in personal terms, unless they're wearing a really hideous outfit—ugh, what were they thinking?!

Rule #2: Take time to think before responding

Oftentimes, we say things in the heat of the moment that we later come to regret. If somebody sends you an email that feels aggressive or accusatory, instead of responding right away, take a step back, go outside for some fresh air, get in your car, drive away, and never come back.

Rule #3: Don't vent to your coworkers

It might be tempting to air your professional (or personal) grievances to somebody in the workplace, but even if you trust them, it's a bad idea. Not only is there a risk that your comments will be repeated, there's also a good chance that nobody wants to hear about your ferret's gluten sensitivity.

Rule #4: Know how to change the subject

In the event that a coworker starts discussing gossip with you, you should know how to smoothly change the subject back to something professional. Try saying: "I'm sorry, but this project requires a lot of focus," or "Did you know that Czechoslovakia was split into two sovereign states in 1993?"

Rule #5: Don't repeat anything you might have heard

Despite your best intentions, you might occasionally overhear some office gossip. If this happens, make sure you don't repeat what you've heard, as this could draw you into the controversy. Instead, write down exactly what you heard in the bathroom stall to keep the rumor going.

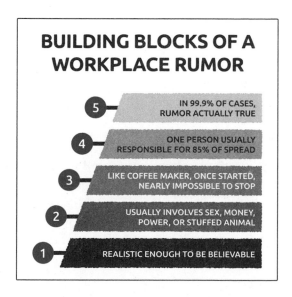

BUT WHAT IF YOU LIKE DRAMA?

There's a reason why conflict-laden reality shows are so popular: some people are naturally drawn to drama. It's quite possible that you're one of those people and believe that leaning into workplace drama might make the job more fun and exciting.

How to start drama

In the event that a drama-filled workplace is what you're looking for, here are some tips to help you turn your workplace into a daytime soap opera:

1. Position yourself as a great listener so coworkers become comfortable telling you their thoughts and secrets, then spread those secrets generously throughout the workplace.
2. Create a fake social media profile and send friend requests to coworkers in order to dig up revealing personal information.
3. If a coworker asks you for advice, intentionally give suggestions that are likely to backfire and create more controversy.
4. When a rumor appears to be dying down, reignite it by adding an additional (made-up) element.
5. "Accidentally" forward any controversial emails to the person who is being discussed.

The effects of workplace drama

It might seem like it's all fun and games, but workplace drama can have serious implications for company culture and detrimental effects on workplace morale. Workplace drama can cause some or all of the following:

- increased stress
- higher turnover
- reduced productivity
- decreased boredom
- an uptick in pressing your ear against the conference room door to get a better listen
- increase in the quality of stories to tell your significant other when you get home from work

FINAL THOUGHTS

If there weren't millions of workers who thrived on drama, then it wouldn't be so prevalent in the workplace today. The sad truth is that for many people, drama can make work less tedious and more exciting, at the expense of their coworkers' well-being, of course.

The good news is that unlike your complete lack of any marketable skills, it's never too late to avoid workplace gossip. Make it a point to remain professional at work and you won't get drawn into petty feuds. If you decide to go in the other direction, however, do so at your own risk. And always remember: there are far more lucrative ways to alienate everybody you work with.

The Rules of the Kitchen: Stealing Someone's Yogurt Is Literally a Crime

There is, perhaps, no other place where proper etiquette is as important as the kitchen or break room. Unlike the bathroom, we don't have individual feeding stalls, so respecting people's boundaries and adhering to the unspoken rules of the kitchen is tantamount to a smooth workplace experience.

When people are hungry, they can turn into rabid animals, which makes it that much more important to be considerate when secretly eating someone else's food. So whether you brought your lunch from home (unlikely) or spent thirty dollars on a greasy sub from the quirky sandwich shop up the street, make sure you follow the rules of the kitchen.

Here are some basic workplace kitchen rules to get you started:

Rule #1: Keep it clean
Always try to leave the kitchen a bit cleaner than you found it, which, if you've seen a typical workplace break room, shouldn't be too difficult. Pick up after yourself, empty the coffee maker after using it, and wipe down the oil from the burrito you threw at the wall in a sudden fit of rage.

Rule #2: Don't consume other people's food

While those two slices of sausage-and-mushroom pizza might look a lot more appealing than your damp, pitiful excuse for a tuna sandwich, it is literally a crime to steal somebody else's food. Only after a week has gone by does an untouched food item legally become fair game.

Rule #3: Don't leave uneaten food in the fridge

While most of us lack the basic self-control to eat the food we've brought from home for more than two days in a row, this doesn't give you an excuse to leave your dry, uneaten grilled chicken and brown rice sitting in a cloudy plastic container for an entire election cycle. Take it home or throw it out. Just get rid of it before the hazmat team has to come in.

Rule #4: Label food that belongs to you

While you might be willing to follow local and federal laws, this doesn't mean your ravenous coworkers will, so make sure to label all food that belongs to you unless you're willing to share. It might help to add a thinly veiled threat under your name, though neither of these will guarantee compliance.

Rule #5: Be mindful of extremely odorous food

A piece of fish can make for a tasty meal. However, subjecting your coworkers to its lingering smell for the rest of the afternoon won't endear you to anyone. So be mindful of food that has strong, abiding smells. The only thing allowed to linger in the workplace all day is tension.

Rule #6: Don't take up too much storage space

Food and supplies can accumulate quickly, so try not to use more than your fair share of storage space in the fridge and kitchen cabinets. If something doesn't need to be refrigerated, keep it at your desk instead, right next to the bottle of cognac.

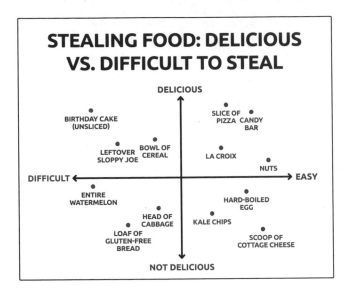

EATING AT YOUR DESK

On occasion, you might want to eat alone at your desk. Whether it's because you don't have time for a break or because the thought of spending another minute with your coworkers fills you with immeasurable despair, no matter the reason, when eating at your desk, there are still rules you need to follow.

- Ask for permission. Some workplaces won't allow you to eat at your desk, so be ready to make up a fake illness to justify your position.
- Time your meal so that it corresponds with everybody's lunch break. The repulsive sounds of you loudly chewing your pita chips at 10:15 a.m. are unlikely to make you any new friends.
- Expect interruptions from coworkers, who will hover over you and stare at your food with heavy, covetous eyes.
- Try not to make a mess. Food can leave bacteria on your computer and keyboard, so make sure to disinfect after each meal

or just swap out your equipment with a coworker's while they're away from their desk.

DECLINING AN OFFER FOR FOOD

If somebody offers you food, you might feel obligated to accept it to avoid being seen as rude or ungrateful (which you are). This, however, can be a mistake. Nobody should be forced to eat something they don't want to eat. Here are some ways to politely decline when somebody offers food you don't want:

- "Thanks so much for offering me a piece of your Bundt cake, but I have a strict rule about avoiding joy in the workplace."
- "I've heard that your lasagna is delicious. However, I prefer foods that are spelled phonetically."
- "It looks like this buffalo chicken dip took a lot of work. It's too bad you don't apply this same level of effort at your job."
- "This must be the pasta salad that everyone always rants and raves about. I assume it tastes *a lot* better than it looks."

FINAL THOUGHTS

Food is known for bringing us together, but in the conflict-laden workplace, it's just as likely to tear us apart. This is why it's so important to follow proper food etiquette, whether you bring your food from home like a pretentious snob or order takeout every day like a slovenly, habitual bachelor.

But don't let our overly prescriptive guidance stop you from enjoying your meal, because in the workplace, that sudden rush of glucose might be the only bright spot in an otherwise bleak day. So eat that cookie . . . heck, eat two. Just make sure to finish it before Katherine from accounting catches you going through her snack drawer.

Apologizing: How to Make It Look Like You're Sorry Without Giving Up Any Power

Despite your best efforts, the workplace frequently creates situations that make it necessary to offer an apology. You might be forced to apologize to your supervisor, to a client, to a coworker, or to your gastroenterologist (though that's a whole other story).

Apologies become necessary due to personal failures (yours are many), on behalf of the company, or as a result of the complexities of office politics. No matter the reason, when offering an apology, there's one important thing to remember: you don't have to be sincere. You just have to say you're sorry without giving up any power.

WHEN TO GIVE AN APOLOGY

The first rule of apologizing is understanding whether an apology is warranted in the first place. The last thing you want is to appear overly kind (weak) to your coworkers, as they will use the opportunity to extract further apologies and subsequently walk all over you.

The following scenarios do not require a formal apology:

- when you've used the last sugar packet
- when a customer has misinterpreted a correctly written email

- when you've reported your employer to the health department for a mold problem
- when your portable space heater is creating a strange smell

However, if you've done any of the following, an apology might be in order:

- when you've shown up late for a meeting and kept your coworkers waiting
- when you've accidentally provided incorrect information to a client or coworker
- when you've purposely provided incorrect information to a client or coworker
- when you've replaced all the meat items in the fridge with their vegan equivalents without permission
- when your false allegations to the Securities and Exchange Commission have caused the company's stock to be delisted from the New York Stock Exchange

HOW TO APOLOGIZE

If it's become clear that an apology is in order, make sure to apologize the correct way. Here's how:

- **Apologize as quickly as possible.** Don't wait too long to issue your apology as a delay might cause hard feelings to develop. An apology neutralizes blowback and immediately and permanently absolves you of all guilt no matter how morally repugnant your behavior was.
- **Acknowledge the impact on others.** Make it clear that you understand how your mistake has affected others, even if you have no clue whatsoever how your mistake has affected anyone at all.

- **Do not shift blame.** Always take full responsibility even if somebody else is involved. This will give you leverage over the other person while making it appear as if you're truly contrite.
- **Don't make excuses.** There are always reasons why you did what you did, but stay away from justifying your own mistakes and stick to pointing out every single mistake made by others.
- **Explain how you intend to fix it.** It's important that you not only apologize but explain what you're doing to remedy the mistake and to ensure that it doesn't happen again. The key here is to describe what you're going to do, not to actually do it.

HOW NOT TO APOLOGIZE

There are many ways to mess up an apology. Here are a few examples:

- "I'm so sorry that you're not able to control your anger like an adult."
- "Please forgive me for assuming you actually had a sense of humor."
- "I hope you'll accept my apology because I really don't feel like talking about this again."
- "I'd like to apologize because it's a lot easier than dealing with you being passive-aggressive for the next three years."
- "I know you usually make bad decisions, but try to make a good one this time and accept my sincere apology."

HOW TO MAINTAIN POWER
AFTER AN APOLOGY

While apologies can help us repair relationships and rebuild trust, they usually come at a cost: diminished power. Coworkers can sense weakness, and there's nothing that screams capitulation quite like saying you're sorry.

Fortunately, there are ways to mitigate the risk of your apology being used against you by your rivals. Here are some tips:

- Compare the act you're apologizing for to something much worse, minimizing its impact.
- Immediately after apologizing, show dominance by starting an argument in front of everyone.
- Avoid ever actually using the word *sorry*.
- If apologizing via email, make the font really small.
- Say "We all have to take responsibility," gaslighting your coworkers into sharing a portion of the blame.
- After apologizing, do the exact same thing you apologized for again.

FORMAL NOTICE OF APOLOGY

TO: _____   FROM: _____

CURRENT LEVEL OF GUILT (CHECK ONE):

☐ SIGNIFICANT   ☐ ABOVE AVERAGE   ☐ MIDDLING   ☐ LOW   ☐ SOCIOPATH

I WOULD LIKE TO APOLOGIZE FOR ____[OFFENDING BEHAVIOR]____. IT'S CLEAR THAT MY

ACTIONS COULD BE SEEN AS __[PROBLEMATIC, OFFENSIVE, DISGRACEFUL]__. I NEVER INTENDED

TO __[HURT, OFFEND, STEAL FROM]__ YOU, AND AM DEEPLY ____[HUMAN EMOTION]____ OF

THE WAY I BEHAVED. THIS HAS BEEN A LEARNING EXPERIENCE, AND I INTEND TO

[THING YOU HAVE NO INTENTION OF DOING].

SINCERELY, _____

ALTERNATIVES TO APOLOGIZING

In the event that your fragile ego and warped sense of self prevent you from apologizing, there are some alternatives. These may come with their own consequences, so be sure to understand the risks.

1. **Doubling down.** Instead of admitting you were wrong, this approach allows you to stay the course, learning nothing and not giving an inch.
2. **Lashing out.** This approach involves flailing in anger at everything around you, ensuring your irrational response to being called out distracts from the original transgression.
3. **Playing the victim.** When taking this approach, it's important to throw in anecdotes about going through difficult times in order to be seen as more sympathetic.
4. **Shifting responsibility.** When attempting to blame others for your own mistakes, make sure to pick a believable scapegoat. This will add credibility to your claims and likely create enough doubt to get you off the hook.

FINAL THOUGHTS

While no one likes to apologize, in the workplace sometimes apologies become necessary. No matter who you are or how high up the totem pole you make it, there's a good chance that at some point in your career, you'll have to say you're sorry (unless your father owns the company). The key is to do it with humility, grace, and with the best acting you can possibly muster—pretend you're trying to win an Oscar.

But if you find yourself having to apologize frequently, you might want to consider whether *you're* the problem, before quickly ruling that out and concluding that it must be everybody else. After all, we don't go to work to reflect on our shortcomings; we go to work because it's literally the only way to avoid abject poverty and despair.

Navigating Social Events and What to Do If You Drank Too Much

Whether it's the company holiday party or an after-hours barbecue at a coworker's house, social events are a common occurrence in the modern workplace. These occasions can be a great way to blow off steam and get to know the people you work with in a more informal setting. But they can also carry risks, as the loose, permissive nature of social events can bring out the person you swore you left behind in college.

Though a work-related gathering might feel more social than professional, it's important to be on your best behavior, because what happens outside of work won't stay outside of work for long, no matter how many pinkie promises or blood oaths you've made. A good rule of thumb is if you wouldn't do it in the workplace, then you shouldn't do it at a social event, which probably rules out having a good time.

GROUND RULES FOR SOCIAL EVENTS

When attending an event, it's important to understand the basic rules, which can help you avoid trouble and ensure your reputation doesn't get any worse than it already is.

Rule #1: Dress appropriately

You don't need to wear the same thing you wear to the office, but make sure you don't overdo (or underdo) it. Dress for the occasion. If it's a formal event, dust off the suit and tie; if it's an exorcism, make sure to bring an all-black cassock.

Rule #2: Don't drink too much

If alcohol is being served at an event, make sure to pace yourself and know your limits. Many a career has been ruined because somebody drank to excess in front of their coworkers rather than take prescription medication, which is more difficult to spot.

Rule #3: Don't hit on your coworkers

Mingling with coworkers in a new setting may cause you to see people in a different light, but it's always a bad idea to hit on a coworker at a social event. Not only do you run the risk of making somebody feel uncomfortable (or worse, harassed), but you might get turned down and never fully recover.

Rule #4: Avoid inappropriate jokes

When you're letting loose, it might be tempting to indulge in humor that wouldn't be appropriate in the workplace. But before cracking that joke, be mindful that these are still your coworkers, who are complete stiffs and who have no sense of humor at all (they think *Friends* is funny).

Rule #5: Don't bring uninvited guests

If your company allows you to bring a plus-one, great. But if not, it's inappropriate to bring someone who wasn't invited. Similarly, it's wise to double-check and make sure that *you* were actually invited too.

Rule #6: Don't hound the execs

Some people use company events as an opportunity to ingratiate themselves to company leadership in an effort to accelerate their career. Try to avoid spending too much time chatting up the bigwigs. Say hello, shake hands, then move on and spend the rest of the evening staring at them from across the room.

Rule #7: Don't talk shop

While it might be tempting to talk about work, social events should be social. Your coworkers are unlikely to appreciate being sucked into another workplace discussion while they're trying to unwind. Stick to lighthearted topics such as the music playlist or the impending collapse of the global food chain.

DECLINING TO ATTEND AN EVENT

Some people prefer not to attend events, deciding that forty hours spent with their coworkers is enough. If the potential of free food and tense, awkward conversation doesn't appeal to you, then you might want to decline your invitation. Here's how to do so without drawing too much attention to yourself:

- Thank the person or people who sent the invitation.
- Indicate that you would have loved to attend.
- Make up a *believable* excuse for why you can't make it, which rules out claiming that you're going on a date.
- Say that you hope everybody has a great time (more likely if you're not there).
- Lie and claim that you'll definitely make it to the next one.

WHAT TO DO IF YOU DRANK TOO MUCH

It's possible that despite your best efforts, you might accidentally drink too much during an event. If this happens, don't panic, since the only way to get rid of a panic attack is with another drink. Instead, take a deep breath and do these five things:

1. **Stop drinking immediately.** Even if you're holding a full drink, put it on a table, dump it into the sink, or toss it into the face of Paul from sales.
2. **Sit down and relax.** Take a seat somewhere quiet so you can try to sober up. If anyone asks, you can say you're not feeling well because you hate being around people you work with.
3. **Don't engage with coworkers.** Now is not the time to get into conversations with others. If somebody tries to engage you, just pretend as if you're on a phone call. Don't make the pretend phone call a discussion about how absolutely wasted you are.
4. **Drink some water.** Alcohol can cause you to become dehydrated, so make sure to drink H2O like your job depends on it, which probably isn't much of a motivator.
5. **Exit safely and gracefully.** If you're unable to sober up quickly, order an Uber or get a ride home from somebody who hasn't been drinking. Try to leave quietly and gracefully, because everybody is watching you . . . right now, they're watching you! Don't trip now.

FINAL THOUGHTS

Letting loose with coworkers at an event can be a lot of fun, and as long as you're careful never to be your true self, you shouldn't have any problems. Use social events as an opportunity to deepen workplace bonds, then use those bonds for your own benefit—it's the fastest way to get ahead.

But always remember that the workplace doesn't end at the office entrance; it follows you to your car, to your bedroom, and yes, to the holiday party. And no matter how many quirky outfits they wear, or how many offhand casual comments they make, keep in mind that your coworkers aren't there to be your friends; they're there because, like you, they don't want to get fired.

STAGES OF DRINKING AT A COMPANY EVENT

ONE DRINK
I'M JUST GONNA HAVE ONE DRINK.
NO BIG DEAL.

TWO DRINKS
WHOA, MY COWORKERS ARE ACTUALLY
KIND OF FUN. WHO KNEW?

THREE DRINKS
TIME TO HIT THE DANCE FLOOR AND
SHOW EVERYONE MY MOVES!

FOUR DRINKS
YOU KNOW WHAT, I'M GONNA TELL MATT
THAT I DON'T APPRECIATE WHAT HE SAID
AT THE MARKETING MEETING.

FIVE DRINKS
NO ONE CAN TELL THAT I'VE
BEEN CRYING, RIGHT?

SIX DRINKS
LOOK AT ALL THESE JERKS HAVING FUN...
LAUGH IT UP, YOU PHONIES.

SEVEN DRINKS
OH GOD, I'M GONNA HAVE TO USE
A SICK DAY TOMORROW.

PART 3

Coworkers
(Getting Along with Your Fellow Inmates)

Without your coworkers, the workplace would be an empty, quiet place, devoid of personalities, challenges, and relationships, leaving you alone to ponder your thoughts without the benefits of mutual support. But enough about your dream life—because the modern workplace is *filled* with coworkers, who now have direct, unfettered access to you at all hours of the day thanks to the magic of smartphones and direct messaging.

This is why your relationship with your coworkers is so important: the people you work with have the potential to make your professional life miserable or to make it *really* miserable, and all of it will depend on how well you manage to get along. In the workplace, you function as part of a team, one spoke in a wheel, one drop of discount soap slowly running down a gas-station bathroom sink. Play your cards right, and your coworkers will have your back. But make a mistake, and you'll have to look over your shoulder, as your workmates will be angling to take you down.

What follows is an attempt to define workplace relationships to help you build lasting bonds with your professional peers. Developing true connections with coworkers can help you advance in your career. But neglecting to do so can lead to isolation and stagnant prospects, so make sure you choose wisely. After all, you don't have much of a choice about who you get to work with, but you *do* get to choose whether you get along with them or not. So put your ego aside and—oh, who are we kidding here? Just try not to get fired, okay?

How to Find a Workplace Friend and Make a Workplace Enemy, Even If You're 100 Percent Remote

Building relationships in the workplace is never easy—there are always so many variables that come into play. A coworker's seniority, their trustworthiness, and their compensation as it relates to yours must all be factored in when deciding whether to trust somebody with your deepest, darkest secrets (we know what you did).

Workplace friendship, therefore, is a journey, not a destination. Somebody might start off being your friend, then later become an enemy, before teaming back up with you to help take down somebody you both despise—it's all quite Machiavellian. So buckle down, put on your fakest smile, and get ready to make some workplace friends, likely to be outnumbered by your workplace enemies.

TIPS FOR MAKING FRIENDS AT WORK

Making friends at work can be more difficult than it was at school, because your parents can't just pay people to hang out with you anymore. But if you don't make a connection right away, don't fret, since it usually takes time for people to warm up to their new colleagues. Here are some tips that might help:

1. Introduce yourself

Don't be shy about introducing yourself to coworkers. Start a conversation and ask which department they work in, how long they've been with the company, and whether they are on a diet. Small talk can break the ice and help get the ball rolling toward friendship.

2. Commit random acts of kindness

Doing generous things, such as buying food for your teammates or offering to help a coworker hire a hit man, can endear you to your colleagues and help steer you toward a friendship. Never be bashful about doing things for others.

3. Eat lunch with others

Taking your meals at your desk has its appeal, but if you want to make friends, you need to leave your comfort zone and join others for lunch, whether in the break room or at a local restaurant. And if you really want to impress your coworkers, eat *their* lunch too.

4. Try to be approachable

If your coworkers see that you're interesting and approachable, they're more likely to strike up a conversation. Try decorating your desk with conversation-starting items, such as pictures of your pets, pop-culture knickknacks, or the haunted ashes of an ancient crow, and it's likely somebody will chat you up.

5. Attend events and join company groups

Most companies offer opportunities to interact outside the workplace, whether it's company outings or volunteer or recreation groups. Use these as opportunities to connect with coworkers or to fall and get injured so you can stay home while getting paid by the company's insurance provider.

6. Learn people's names

In today's fast-paced world, many people don't take the time to remember others' names. Doing so can set you apart and will show that you're interested in your coworkers. The best way to remember someone's name is to repeat it to yourself before going into the break room and screaming it at the top of your lungs.

7. Bond over common interests

People tend to connect over shared interests, so it might be worthwhile to start an email thread or a Slack channel about a topic you and a coworker(s) find interesting, such as sports, a TV series, or the various ways you could get your manager charged with a crime. Just be mindful to keep conversations in the workplace professional at all times.

8. Become a good listener

Most people appreciate a good listener, so honing your ability to listen can pay dividends in workplace friendships. Not only that, but you can also use people's secrets as fodder for a dramatic workplace tell-all, which—if marketed properly—can make you enough money to allow you to quit.

9. Use blackmail

Trying to kindle workplace friendships is difficult when you don't have some sort of competitive edge. This is why good old-fashioned blackmail can be so effective. Find a coworker's weakness, let them know you're willing to exploit it unless they acquiesce to your demands, and you'll have a workplace friend for life.

10. Be yourself

At the end of the day, you should always lead with your authentic self, because pretending to be somebody else is likely to backfire. If you can't show people the true you, then you're unlikely to ever develop lasting friendships. Keep in mind that when we say the "true you" and your "authentic self," we mean the well-crafted, marketable, artificial version of yourself, not your *actual* self, which is someone you definitely want to keep hidden away forever.

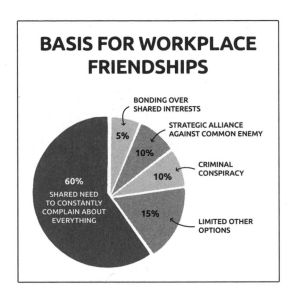

THE DOWNSIDES OF A WORKPLACE FRIENDSHIP

Unfortunately, workplace friendships aren't all flowers and rainbows. In fact, getting too close to people in the workplace can be so precarious that many people make it a point to set boundaries. Here's why:

- Workplace friendships can lead to distractions at work.
- Becoming friends with somebody will limit your ability to use them as a pawn in your sinister workplace machinations.
- It will become more difficult to avoid paying back any money you've borrowed.
- It can lead to your personal secrets being exposed at work.

THE ALTERNATIVE:
A WORKPLACE ENEMY

If you find making friends at work too difficult, or just prefer the drama of having an office nemesis, then making a workplace enemy is an excellent way to go. But you can't just pick a random stranger to be your antagonist. You need to choose wisely, and make sure your long-simmering conflict gets off on the right foot.

Tips for making enemies at work:

1. Pick the right enemy
When picking a workplace enemy, don't be hasty. You're better off taking the time to find the right person to hate rather than jumping in and picking the first person you come across. Look for people who are arrogant, impatient, and lazy—basically, look for people who are a lot like you.

2. Create conflict
Unlike a friend, an enemy is quite easy to make. All you need to do is make them angry, and after that, refuse to apologize—simple! Some ideas for enraging a chosen colleague: accuse them of doing shoddy work (projection), make up an obvious lie, or take credit for something they worked on. After you've set things in motion, just sit back and let their anger simmer.

3. Never make enemies with your supervisor
Do *not* become enemies with your supervisor or with anyone else who has the power to fire you. As fun as it might seem, your adversarial relationship will be short lived, and you'll end up having to look for another job. The *only* exception to this rule is when you're purposely creating conflict in an effort to take over your supervisor's job. But if you attempt this, always remember: "If you come at the king, you best not miss."

4. Use every opportunity to make yourself look good

Workplace rivalries have a tendency to drag other coworkers in, so make sure you use every opportunity to make yourself look like the aggrieved party. Some great ways to do this are by treating everybody who isn't your enemy with special attention and care, and by never bad-mouthing your enemy in front of anybody else. This will make you seem like a considerate and thoughtful person and make it more likely that your coworkers take your side.

5. Focus on the little things

The best way to keep a feud going is to use small opportunities to needle your enemy, as these small slights tend to have an outsized effect. Whether it's unnecessarily copying a supervisor when responding to an email from your enemy or bringing up a past mistake they've made during a team meeting, it's the small details that can keep conflict alive and well.

6. Always disagree

One of the best ways to make (and keep) an enemy at work is to always disagree with their position. This doesn't mean you have to be aggressive about it; in fact, you can be extremely polite, but the key is to make sure you voice disagreement with *every single* position they state out loud, no matter how trivial, obvious, or correct it might be.

7. Scapegoat whenever possible

One of the most useful benefits of having a workplace nemesis is that you can blame them for anything that goes wrong. This becomes especially useful when you're the one who's screwed up, as you can seamlessly assign blame while deflecting attention away from yourself. To be sure, you have to be strategic about it and can't pawn off a mistake that obviously belongs to you. But with the right archenemy, and with enough coworkers on board, it could be smooth sailing for you and rocky waters for your foe.

TEAMING UP WITH AN ENEMY
FOR A GREATER CAUSE

On (rare) occasions, it might become necessary to join forces with an enemy when you're both faced with an outside threat or when an opportunity for mutual advancement arrives. Coming together is usually easier than it seems, especially if your rival understands the benefits of putting your differences aside to get something done.

But be careful, because your enemy is unlikely to let bygones be bygones for long (and neither should you). A workplace enemy is an enemy for life; the only question is whether the lingering contempt is overt or bubbling just beneath the surface. In any case, always keep one eye open, one hand on your wallet, and the other hand ready to type up a false accusation.

FINAL THOUGHTS

Establishing friendships with coworkers can make your professional life easier, more rewarding, and can help you weather the difficult times that inevitably accompany any career. These friendships can also be shamelessly exploited for your personal gain, whether through manipulative political jockeying, as a smoke screen to hide your professional shortcomings, or in more simple ways: like having somebody buy you coffee more times than you've bought it for them.

Similarly, a workplace enemy can be extremely useful if you're cunning enough to leverage your discord in the right way. Being able to maintain a steady antagonistic relationship is what separates the successful people from everybody else, and being unafraid to offend people for no reason whatsoever is a great way to break into upper management.

So, whether you decide to make a friend or an enemy, make sure you do it with aplomb. Because in the workplace, you never want to go it alone.

The Different Types of Coworkers

One of the virtues of the modern workplace is that it brings all sorts of people together. Everybody from the poor to the rich, the nerds to the jocks, from the introverts to the extroverts are all thrown together in one smoldering cauldron of frayed nerves—what could possibly go wrong?!

After you spend years grinding out a living, you'll start to notice patterns among your coworkers. Different personas that—while they might have their own unique characteristics—usually fall into a handful of easily identifiable archetypes. Since you're the type of person who will do anything and everything (short of working hard) to advance your career, it behooves you to understand the different types of coworkers, and to figure out which one of the categories you fall into.

While not exhaustive, the following list covers the different types of coworkers you're likely to encounter at work. Some coworkers might fit into more than one category—*definitely* stay away from these people.

THE POSITIVITY PUSHER

This is one of the most annoying types of coworkers, although they do have some redeeming qualities. The Positivity Pusher has bought into the toxic positivity movement hook, line, and sinker and believes in seizing the day and always looking on the bright side of things, no matter how much evidence there is to the contrary. The Positivity Pusher is the type of coworker who will accost you at the coffee machine before you're fully awake to extol the warm weather and to wish you "another great day," and will *never* send an email without a handful of exclamation points or smiley-face emojis. Although the Positivity Pusher means well, dealing with them day in and day out can be extremely exhausting.

THE KEEPER OF SECRETS

At the opposite end of the spectrum is the Keeper of Secrets, who would sooner die than reveal anything about themselves. The Keeper of Secrets believes there should be a separation between their personal and professional lives. However, they tend to take this to the extreme, refusing to open up to anyone, and clamming up whenever discussions of a personal nature arise. What is the Keeper of Secrets hiding? Are they in the Witness Protection Program? Do they live a quirky, unconventional life? Unless you follow them home from work, you'll never know, because the Keeper of Secrets plays their cards close to their chest.

THE COMPLAINER

Every workplace has at least one complainer, and some workplaces have many. This type of coworker is adept at finding a problem for every solution and isn't shy about sharing it with everyone else. The Complainer might be a semi-competent employee, but they more than make up for it with their incessant whining and negativity. In fact, the Complainer is so skilled at spreading negativity that whenever another employee starts spending time with them, they quickly become a Complainer too. The Complainer is like a black hole of pessimism, devouring everything in its path. And don't bother trying to cheer up this coworker, because there's nothing that makes the Complainer happier than being unhappy.

THE OVERACHIEVER

This type of coworker is every employer's dream. Not only is the Overachiever a hard worker, but they will almost never turn down more work, no matter how swamped they might already be. Why does the Overachiever work so hard? Did they inherit their work ethic from their parents? Is it because they have no boundaries, not even for their ambition? Or is it simply the only way they know to stave off the pervasive and unbearable sense of impending doom? Who knows! The Overachiever is too busy working to give you an answer. But if you want someone on your team who will pick up your slack and then some, the Overachiever is the only logical choice.

THE SCHEMER

This type of coworker is just as likely to end up a multimillionaire as they are to be indicted for a series of financial crimes. The Schemer has plenty of energy but tends to talk in a whisper, constantly pitching ridiculous schemes that promise to make them rich, no matter how absurd or illegal they might be. There is no fleeting trend that the Schemer won't latch onto, whether it's cryptocurrency, the keto diet, or yoga pants for dogs. This type of coworker tends to be charismatic, prevaricating, and is almost always male. And while they might be extremely entertaining, be careful about getting too close to the Schemer, because they'll take you for every penny you've got and then some.

THE MOST AVERAGE PERSON ALIVE

If you are hoping to be fascinated, intellectually stimulated, or inspired, then you've come to the wrong place. The Most Average Person Alive has almost no memorable qualities except, of course, their unmitigated mediocrity. This type of coworker is neither exceptional nor deficient, neither an asset nor a liability. In fact, the Most Average Person Alive is able to weather most workplace storms precisely because they inspire so little reaction one way or another. To be fair, this type of coworker does keep the economy afloat, both as an employee and a consumer. But a striver they are not, and unless you're looking to coast, doing the same exact job for the next forty years, you never want to become the Most Average Person Alive.

THE DRAMA GENERATOR

No matter how boring a company might be, within weeks, this coworker will easily turn it into a carnival of backstabbing and intrigue. The Drama Generator thrives on interpersonal chaos and uses exploitative reality TV as an actual guide for how people are supposed to behave. And if you thought that turmoil as a way of life would hurt someone's career prospects, guess again, because the Drama Generator can easily position themselves for promotion, using the same treachery they use to turn the workplace into a sordid den of confrontation. If you are unlucky enough to get stuck with one of these demented types, try to keep your distance. Otherwise, you'll find yourself being accused, exposed, and possibly arrested—all to serve the Drama Generator's perverse machinations.

THE ELITIST

If you would like a constant reminder of your inability to get into an Ivy League school, the Elitist won't disappoint. This type of coworker will probably be in management, will probably be polite, and will probably have dead eyes—their soul having been slowly excised through years of high-intensity coursework and long, Cobb sandwich–fueled discussions with their distinguished uncle Whittaker Barrington III on the deck of the local country club. The Elitist is nice enough, but both of you will always know that you're from different worlds. And if the time comes when the company has to do layoffs, you can be absolutely sure that it'll be you, and not the Elitist, on the chopping block.

THE HOT MESS

There is no organizational process on earth that can restore order to this coworker's life. The Hot Mess is perpetually late, constantly confused, and pathologically disorganized. And no matter how hard they try, they can't go a day without absentmindedly forgetting to do something important. Mismatched socks? Check. Taking up two parking spots at once? Check. A huge coffee stain on their shirt? Check. The Hot Mess will show up to a meeting twenty minutes late, then proceed to give a presentation meant for somebody else. It's impossible to know what's going on in this coworker's mind, but you can bet that, if nothing else, it, too, is a bit of a mess.

THE DELEGATOR

A self-described "natural leader," the Delegator has never met an assignment they didn't immediately try to pass on to someone else. This type of coworker frequently ends up in management, where they assign tasks left and right without a moment's thought as to their own meager workload. Try to challenge the Delegator's efforts and you'll get an earful about company hierarchy and the importance of being a team player. But the Delegator fancies themselves a general, not a foot soldier; so, no matter how hard you try, you won't be able to convince them to get into the trenches and do any actual work.

FINAL THOUGHTS

Try as we might, there's no real way to separate ourselves from the myriad of colorful personalities we'll encounter at work. Like an overbearing neighbor, our coworkers are forced upon us, and it's up to us to learn how to coexist or to turn to a life of crime, which, from what we understand, can actually be quite lucrative. In any case, try to remember that everyone is just doing their best (to avoid each other), and make sure to lead with compassion, or at least make it seem like that's what you're doing.

And while it might be tempting to look for flaws in others, always remember that you have your own flaws too. Many, many flaws. Hundreds, perhaps thousands of flaws, big and small. You're covered in flaws. Flaws everywhere. It's actually kind of crazy how flawed you are. But don't worry, because with enough effort, misdirection, and blame, you can make sure that no one else notices any of your (there are so many) flaws.

Boundaries and Why You Should Never Trust Rick from Sales

The relationships you develop at work can be impactful, but there are many ways in which they will differ from relationships in your personal life. Since the workplace has so many rules, both spoken and non, it's important to set and follow boundaries, lest you find yourself stuck in an unpleasant situation from which you can't escape (in addition to the unpleasant situation of being stuck at work, from which you also can't escape).

Setting healthy boundaries can also protect you from being taken advantage of by your employer. In today's interconnected world, many companies expect you to be at their beck and call twenty-four hours a day. Without boundaries, you may never get a reprieve from your company's oppressive grasp. You will be stuck in an endless loop of saying yes to new assignments, when you'd rather spend your time trying to trick somebody into a relationship online.

HOW TO SET BOUNDARIES

Setting boundaries can be tricky. Here are some tips that might help:

1. Understand your own boundaries first
Before setting boundaries, make sure you understand where you want to draw the line. People have their own priorities, so it can

help to identify and map out what you are, and aren't, comfortable with. Pay attention to situations that make you feel uncomfortable, angry, or stressed out, like having to work on Fridays or being forced to respond to emails. Once you have an inventory, you can focus on setting limits.

2. Communicate your limits

After you've identified where to draw the line, you need to let other people know. There's no need to make a big production out of it; you can simply send an email or a group message. For instance, if you don't want to answer emails after 5:00 p.m., threaten to plant a damaging story about your coworkers in a trade publication if they don't respect your wishes. Communication is key, so make sure to get your message across clearly and effectively.

3. Don't be afraid to say no

Many of us have a hard time saying no, whether it's out of guilt or out of a fear of losing our jobs. But turning down projects, tasks, or invitations is perfectly acceptable. In fact, in many cases, it can mean the difference between a pleasant work-life balance and an unmanageable schedule. To get better at saying no, practice doing it in your everyday life. Walk into a store, purchase a product, and when the cashier asks you to pay, look them in the eye and say no, and walk out. Once the initial discomfort wears off, you'll have no problem turning down unwanted requests.

4. Use technology

Although technology is partially responsible for the lack of boundaries in today's workplace, it can also help us to set limits. Used properly, workplace software can let others know when we're unavailable or don't want to be bothered. Get in the habit of setting away messages when you're busy or on vacation and turn off notifications after hours. And if you happen to be technically savvy, you can take it a step further and hack into your company's payroll software and increase your salary by 100 percent. While this won't help with setting boundaries, it will make the work assigned twice as rewarding.

5. Get ready for pushback

Unfortunately, when we start to set boundaries, we're likely to get negative reactions from people who prefer to keep things the way they were. It's perfectly normal to get pushback, so don't be surprised if your manager or coworkers try to pressure you to drop your demands. This, however, is when you have to stay strong and insist that your boundaries are nonnegotiable, unless there's a large sum of cash involved. We all have our price, so don't compromise your morals unless you're being paid a hefty sum. After all, you can't put a price on integrity, until you get into the six-figure range.

HOW TO DEAL WITH PEOPLE WHO WON'T RESPECT YOUR BOUNDARIES

Even when you've clearly established boundaries and communicated them to your coworkers, there are likely to be people who refuse to respect your limits. When this happens, here's what you can do:

- Restate your boundaries and make it clear that they're nonnegotiable.
- Don't back down. You're the one in charge of your boundaries, so don't let anyone convince you otherwise.
- Document everything. Take detailed notes every time someone violates your boundaries. Take notes on what they're wearing and what they had for lunch. Document their bathroom breaks. Be thorough.
- Turn the tables by violating *their* boundaries. Get extremely close when talking to them. Squeeze their sandwich bread. Email their secrets to the entire department.

- Make a scene. Wait until there are lots of people around, then proceed to have a complete meltdown in front of everyone.
- If all else fails, report the person to HR. Make sure the infractions sound much worse than they really are. If needed, make up an elaborate version of what really happened. Don't be afraid to use your imagination.

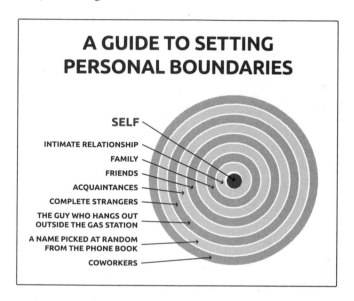

A GUIDE TO SETTING PERSONAL BOUNDARIES

SELF
INTIMATE RELATIONSHIP
FAMILY
FRIENDS
ACQUAINTANCES
COMPLETE STRANGERS
THE GUY WHO HANGS OUT
OUTSIDE THE GAS STATION
A NAME PICKED AT RANDOM
FROM THE PHONE BOOK
COWORKERS

WHY YOU SHOULD NEVER TRUST RICK FROM SALES

Boundaries can help protect us from being exploited, but they can also help put distance between ourselves and our less trustworthy coworkers. These are the types of people who have no qualms about throwing us under the bus if it suits their ends. Despite what you may think, you can be sure there are at least a few people like this where you work—people like Rick from sales.

To be clear, we're not trying to pick on sales. Rick is simply a literary representation of an untrustworthy coworker. He could just as easily be Jane from fulfillment or Mike from customer support.

But what all of these (hypothetical) coworkers have in common is that they're not to be trusted. Given the opportunity, they'll ruin our jobs and our lives, and won't lose a wink of sleep.

Here's how you can tell that you're dealing with potential "Ricks":

- When you first meet them, they ask lots of personal questions.
- They always seem to be involved in other people's personal business.
- Before joining your company, they were forced to resign from their position as mayor of Cincinnati due to a corruption scandal.
- They try to dominate every conversation, which is annoying since that's what you're trying to do.
- They are charismatic and overly charming but repeatedly turn you down when you ask them out on a date.
- Instead of taking responsibility, they blame others, which makes trying to sabotage their career extremely difficult.

FINAL THOUGHTS

If you fail to plan, then you plan to fail. Or is it "If you plan to fail, you fail to plan"? Who knows! Either way, you should *plan* to keep your coworkers at arm's length if you want to avoid ending up in an uncomfortable situation. And the best way to do that is by establishing clear boundaries—which you will never actually enforce because you, at your core, are a moral coward.

But at a minimum, setting boundaries can show your coworkers that you're at work *to work*, not to make friends or to try to enhance your social life. Boundaries, therefore, can be used as signals to make it look like you're a hardworking professional, focused on your tasks and responsibilities. And, as we all know, appearances are everything. So set your boundaries, then kick back and relax. You've earned it.

Walking on Eggshells: The Manager–Employee Relationship

For anyone (un)lucky enough to be employed, there is, perhaps, no more important relationship than the one with their supervisor. Managers hold a great deal of sway over the people they're in charge of, setting expectations for our day-to-day responsibilities, serving as gatekeepers for raises and promotions, and giving us crippling anxiety with their constant and ever-evolving mood swings. A good manager can make work life tolerable, while a bad one has the potential to turn you into a full-fledged communist.

Navigating the relationship with your supervisor can be tricky, but it needn't be impossible. Managers, despite their confident outward demeanor, are people, just like you and me. They put their pants on one leg at a time, unless they know how to do that cool jumping move where they can put both legs in at once. In any event, maintaining a good relationship with your supervisor should always be a top priority, because the alternative is significantly worse. Not like, *death* worse, but still pretty bad.

• • •

TIPS FOR IMPROVING YOUR
RELATIONSHIP WITH YOUR BOSS

They're there, you're there, why not make the most of it? Here are some ways you can keep the relationship with your manager on the up and up:

1. Schedule frequent one-on-one meetings

While your brain, heart, and intuition might be telling you to stay as far away from your boss as possible, frequent check-ins can help get you on the same page and strengthen the relationship. You can use these meetings to catch up, get feedback on your performance, and to show them those pictures you took of them cheating on their spouse. Try to schedule meetings on a daily, weekly, or bi-weekly basis.

2. Be responsive

Most supervisors prefer to stay informed, which is why you should always be responsive to emails, messages, and other inquiries from your boss. Some managers might be okay with a monthly update, while others prefer to be apprised weekly, daily, or, in some cases, every hour. Tell them everything: what you're working on, what you had for lunch, why you use that prescription skin cream. Don't hold back.

3. Get to know each other

One of the best ways to build rapport with your manager is by getting to know each other on a personal level. If you can get your manager to feel sorry for you, then they'll have a much harder time reprimanding you or letting you go. Similarly, if you learn more about your boss's personal life and about what makes them tick, you can subtly manipulate them into doing your bidding by playing to their emotions.

4. Treat your boss with respect

People tend to treat others the way they want to be treated, so always show your boss the utmost respect. It doesn't matter if they're a slovenly old fool whose only goal in life is to extract every last bit of lifeblood from their miserable, overworked staff, or that, given the chance, they'd fire you and cut off your only source of income without so much as batting an eye—you have to treat them with respect. Don't ever question it.

5. Own your mistakes

Part of a manager's responsibility is to hold people accountable, so if you're willing to take responsibility for your failures, you'll probably earn some much-needed brownie points. Unfortunately, if you try using those same brownie points to pay rent, or to cover your student loan payments, you'll end up destroying your credit and living on the street. The same goes for kudos, props, and shout-outs—they're all technically worthless.

6. Try to resolve misunderstandings quickly and professionally

Sometimes, things go wrong. It's just the nature of work (and your never-ending string of failures). That's why it's important to address any issues head-on instead of letting them linger. Pull your manager aside privately and confess your sins. Get down on both knees and beg for forgiveness. They are a merciful, compassionate god, and, if you show them that you've repented, they could—maybe, possibly—find it in their heart to forgive you.

7. Maintain a positive attitude

If there's one thing that can endear you to a manager, it's pretending that you're happy. A positive attitude will not only raise the morale among your coworkers; it will also show that you're an engaged, committed employee. To develop a more positive attitude, practice smiling, maintaining a high level of energy, and trying to forget every single unbearably painful thing that has happened (and keeps happening) to you every single day of your life. Your boss will appreciate it.

8. Be someone they can count on

At the end of the day, managers prefer employees who make their lives easier, so it helps to be the kind of person they can reach out to when they're in a pinch. Another, easier alternative is to *say* that you're the type of person they can reach out to when they're in a pinch, despite your obvious unreliability and poor quality of work. But by simply *telling* your manager that they can count on you, you will strengthen the relationship, which is all you were going for anyway.

9. Make them look good

Most managers tend to spend a lot of time thinking about their next promotion. That's why anything you can do to help get them there is likely to score you some points, whether it's making them look good in a meeting, coming up with an idea and letting them take credit for it, or marrying them in order to help them project an air of stability. Remember: it's not about you. It's *always* about them and their needs.

10. Understand what's important to them

Different bosses value different things, so it can help to identify what *your* manager finds important and then focus your energies there. For instance, your manager might put a lot of emphasis on punctuality, in which case, you should try to stay up all night long so you don't oversleep in the morning. Similarly, another manager might value the quality of work over how quickly you can deliver, which means you're definitely not going to last long *there*. Every manager is different, so try to tailor your working style to match what they're looking for.

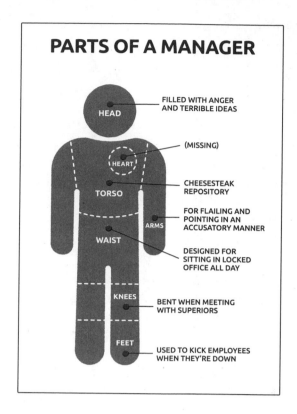

WHAT NOT TO DO

When it comes to maintaining your relationship with your manager, there are some things you should never do. Here are a few:

- Don't contradict your manager in front of others.
- Never assign blame to your manager, even if they're at fault.
- Never lie to your manager unless it's about something really important.
- Avoid going to your manager with your problems too frequently, and just continue burdening your friends and family instead.

- If your manager gives you constructive feedback, wait until they're finished speaking before breaking down in tears.

FINAL THOUGHTS

There is probably no other relationship in the workplace that's more impactful to your day-to-day well-being than the relationship you have with your boss. This is why it's important to stay on top of it and to make them feel like they're a special prince, deserving of constant and unrelenting adulation. A happy boss is a generous boss, and you're going to need all the goodwill you can get when you ask for those two weeks off to go to that furry convention in Nevada next spring.

So make your boss happy every chance you get. Let them know (make them think) they can count on you when the going gets tough. They are, after all, your fearless leader, inspiring you to do your best by firing off passive-aggressive emails from the comfort of their corner office, for which they're paid at least two or three times more than you despite doing even less work (which is certainly no easy feat). But, as with all things work related, there's not a whole lot you can do. So suck it up, put on a big smile, and pretend to be inspired. Who knows! You might actually enjoy it.

Social Media Requests from Coworkers: Friendship or Espionage?

The rise of social media has coincided with a strengthening of community bonds and closer relationships between people who were once alienated by way of time and distance—just kidding, it's been almost entirely all bad. Social media throws another wrench into what is already a complicated workplace question: How much of your personal life should you allow your coworkers to see?

Connecting with coworkers on social media (LinkedIn excluded) comes with some benefits but also some drawbacks. It's important to understand what you're getting yourself into before clicking the "Accept" button on that friend request. If you make the right choice, then everything will be fine, but if you make the wrong one, then you might live to regret your decision, which isn't really anything new for you.

THE UPSIDES OF CONNECTING WITH COWORKERS ON SOCIAL MEDIA

Here are some reasons why you might want to connect with your coworkers on social media:

- It provides an opportunity to develop friendships outside the workplace.
- It can help you build trust with someone you might want on your side.
- You might be invited to more events where you can embarrass yourself in front of everyone.
- It will make it look like you actually have friends.
- It can give you more things to talk about during the week.
- It will give your coworkers a chance to see the fake real you, rather than the fake work you.

THE DOWNSIDES OF CONNECTING WITH COWORKERS ON SOCIAL MEDIA

On the flip side, here are some reasons why you might want to think twice before accepting that friend request:

- Your coworkers will learn more about your personal life than you might be comfortable with.
- They could be fishing for information to use against you at work.
- They will find out you've been lying about all the fun things you've told them you've been doing every weekend.
- They will be able to scroll back and see those photos of you from a few years ago (yikes).
- They will find out the personality you've carefully cultivated at work is much different from the personality you've carefully cultivated among friends.
- They might lose respect for you after seeing you've checked in at a Nickelback concert.

HOW TO POLITELY TURN DOWN A FRIEND REQUEST FROM A COWORKER

If you do get a friend or connection request from a coworker, and you don't feel comfortable connecting with them, here are some ways to turn down the request while remaining friendly and professional:

- Send them a note explaining that you prefer to keep your personal and professional lives separate.
- Pull them aside and tell them you respect them too much to let them see the disgraceful way you've chosen to live your life.
- Immediately delete all of your social media accounts.
- Instead of declining the request, ignore it, and when you see the coworker who sent it, act like nothing happened. They will do the same, and you can maintain this tension-filled existence until one of you either leaves the company or dies.

WHAT IF YOU WANT TO CONNECT WITH SOMEBODY AT WORK?

Sometimes, the tables turn, and you might find yourself eager to connect with one of your coworkers on social media. If this happens, make sure to go about it the right way. Here are some tips:

- Make sure they're not someone you're in charge of, as they might feel forced to accept your friend request.
- Avoid sending requests to people you have (or have had) tensions with at work. This will rule out almost everyone.
- Before sending the request, ask your coworker for permission. If they decline, make sure to respect their decision and immediately begin plotting your revenge.
- Double-check your profile before sending a request. Make sure there isn't anything compromising that could hurt your

standing at work, though how much lower could it possibly go anyway?

- Always remember that other people have their own boundaries too. So, if somebody doesn't want to connect with you, don't take it personally. It's not because you've done anything wrong. It's because of who you are as a person.

SIGNS THAT A FRIEND REQUEST IS ACTUALLY ESPIONAGE

While most people aren't diabolical tacticians, there *are* some people in the workplace who will connect with you simply because they want to dig up dirt. Here are some sure signs that a friend request from a coworker is actually espionage:

- The request is from someone you've had problems with before.
- After sending the request, the person immediately messages you and tells you to "watch your back."

- The person accidentally "likes" a ten-year-old photo of you dressed up as Larry the Cable Guy at a Halloween party.
- The friend request comes immediately after you and the person just finished screaming at each other in the conference room.
- You've specifically told this person to never, ever, under any circumstances try to connect with you on social media.

FINAL THOUGHTS

Social media adds complexity to workplace dynamics and can create problems that otherwise wouldn't exist. Whether you're a power user who spends endless hours scrolling through mind-destroying news feeds, or just a dabbler who checks in every now and then to see which of your high school friends is back in rehab, connecting with coworkers on social media can give people a glimpse into your personal life, which some people might not be fully comfortable with.

So before you accept (or send) that friend request, ask yourself the following:

- What can people see when they look at my profile?
- Do I want my coworkers knowing so much about me?
- Is it obvious from looking at my social media feed that I'm physically attracted to Shrek?

If you don't like the answers, then the decision is obvious. But if you do, then make sure you understand what you're getting yourself into. Because no matter how friendly or loyal your coworkers might seem, they—like you—are not to be trusted.

Interoffice Dating:
Great Idea, Dumbass

Relationships with coworkers can take all forms, including the romantic variety. We spend so much time with the people at work that sometimes friendships evolve into something more, and friendly greetings and handshakes turn into hugs and kisses and other stuff we can't write about if we want the publisher to pay us for this book. The workplace, therefore, is often the starting point for relationships, marriages, divorces, and, presumably, that weird thing where people live together but sleep in separate beds.

But before you get too excited and delete all of your dating apps, it's important to understand that dating someone you work with is a risky proposition. Not only are you playing at the edges of what the stuffy human resources department will allow, you're also combining your personal and professional lives, which is never something to take lightly. So, if you *are* going to date a coworker, make sure to go into it with your eyes wide open. Otherwise, you might find yourself in a situation that will make your other dating failures look like a walk in the park.

· · ·

THE RULES FOR DATING COWORKERS

If you're brave enough to start a romantic relationship with some-body at work, make sure you minimize the risk of blowback. Here are some rules to follow when dating a coworker:

Rule #1: Check the company's policy on dating

Before you start smooching in the back staircase, make sure you understand your company's rules on workplace relationships—then proceed to break every single one of them. This is America, right? Why should you listen to some jealous human resources staffer who's probably stuck in an unfulfilling marriage and just wants to prevent everyone else from being happy? Rules were meant to be broken, so get out there and do your thing!

Rule #2: Do not date your boss or anyone you're in charge of

Power dynamics can complicate workplace relationships, so make sure to avoid dating someone you work for or someone who works for you. Not only can things quickly go off the rails if the relationship doesn't work out, but if you date your manager, they are likely to find out that all the excuses you've been making to take days off have been made up.

Rule #3: Keep the relationship private

Even if you desperately want to announce that you've finally con-vinced somebody to date you, it's best to keep any relationship with a coworker to yourself. Telling other people merely invites drama and gossip, and might irritate or even make some people uncomfortable. The good thing, however, is that if *you're* involved, no one is likely to be jealous.

Rule #4: Make sure you and your partner are on the same page

When entering into a relationship with a coworker, it's best that you both agree to some predefined ground rules. It can help to discuss how you're going to keep things professional and how you plan to handle the situation if the relationship doesn't work out. This is also the perfect time to prepare your partner for the nuclear meltdown you're going to have if they ever try to dump you.

Rule #5: Keep any disagreements out of the workplace

One of the worst things you can do is bring your relationship problems to work. Keep your personal and professional lives separate, and don't let arguments with your partner seep into the workplace. Your toxic behavior at home should be completely separate from your toxic behavior at work, so make sure your petty jealousies and insatiable need for revenge are motivated by workplace problems, not relationship ones.

Rule #6: Be mindful of flirtatious office communication

If you're dating someone at work, you might be tempted to conduct personal conversations using company communication tools like email or instant messenger. Be mindful that these conversations are probably accessible by your company and could be used against you in a termination proceeding. Thankfully, there are many other things you've done that can be used to fire you, so don't sweat this one too much.

Rule #7: Avoid PDA

Even if you and your partner can't keep your hands off each other, you should avoid gratuitous public displays of affection in the workplace. Not only does hugging, kissing, and touching make coworkers uncomfortable, but it also likely violates company policy. Rather than showing your affection through physical touch, show it by doing something meaningful, like planting drugs in your partner's boss's car and calling the police. There are many ways to show someone that you care.

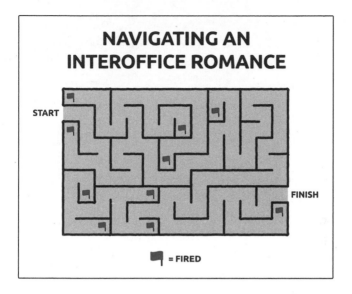

NAVIGATING AN INTEROFFICE ROMANCE

START

FINISH

= FIRED

Rule #8: Expect gossip

No matter how professionally you behave, once your coworkers find out about your relationship, it will become nearly impossible to avoid gossip. Try not to take it personally, since it's human nature to share stories and exaggerations about others, even if those stories happen to be untrue. Instead of trying to stamp out rumors, spread your own rumors about the relationship, making yourself out to be an incredible lover or a secret millionaire. Remember, perception is everything.

Rule #9: Don't force it

Some people will keep a relationship going well past its shelf life because they work with their partner and don't want to deal with the fallout. This is exactly why you must be extra careful before getting into a workplace relationship, and why it's important not to force things if they're not working out. Once your partner has discovered what type of person you *really* are, you probably have days, if not hours, left in the relationship. So don't try to drag it out or you might be putting your job at risk too.

Rule #10: Have an exit plan

Since breakups are usually when things go awry, it can help to have a plan in place beforehand. The best way to go about this is to write down exactly what you're going to do if the relationship ends. You should plan for how you're going to let coworkers know about the breakup, how you'll blame the other person for ruining the relationship, and the exact ways in which you're going to sabotage your ex's career. Once you have a strategy in place, you'll be prepared for the worst.

FINAL THOUGHTS

At the end of the day, before entering into a relationship with a coworker, you should at least be aware of the risks. There are company policies, your coworker's reactions, the possibility that it won't work out, and a whole host of other considerations to take into account. On the other hand, love is blind, and if you find somebody who is willing to look past your numerous shortcomings, then it might be worth the risk.

So don't be afraid to follow your heart, even if it means that your work life will become a bit more complicated. As long as you maintain your professionalism, a consensual relationship between two adults is perfectly normal, no matter what your repressed coworkers might think. But if you decide that it's not worth taking a chance, that's perfectly okay too—just as long as you understand that at the end of the day you're probably going to die alone. Don't say you haven't been warned.

PART 4

Working Remotely
(Wink, Wink)

Recent advances in technology have given us many new experiences, such as the feeling of anxiety at nearly every waking moment, twenty-four hours a day, 365 days a year. These same advances have allowed tens of millions of employees to perform their job duties from home, bringing the workplace to our bedrooms and home offices—a bit creepy if you think about it, isn't it?

For many, remote work has been a godsend, as their taxing morning commute has been replaced by rolling onto their side and tapping the keyboard to make it look like they've logged on for the day. But for others, the prolonged isolation has caused undue distress, and the lack of structure has made it difficult to be productive, which sounds believable enough to garner sympathy if you ever need an excuse for why you haven't done any work.

In the following chapters, we'll offer a detailed plan to help you work remotely without losing your job, your mind, or your laptop, which belongs to the company, so stop using it to download weird stuff, okay? In the end, you might realize the benefits of remote work far outweigh the burdens of the office, or you might just be looking for any excuse to get away from your spouse. Either way, read on.

Getting Out of Your Bed
and Getting into a Routine

One of the more difficult challenges those new to remote work must face is the question of how to structure their day. When we're no longer constrained by the prying eyes of our supervisors and coworkers, the burden falls on us to use our time effectively, and to avoid the temptation to procrastinate, get distracted, and to read books like this all day instead of helping create shareholder value.

Getting into a routine starts with forming good habits. Since you're obviously not going to do that, the next best option is to trick yourself into doing just enough to avoid putting your job in jeopardy.

TIPS FOR SUCCESSFULLY WORKING FROM HOME

While everybody's approach to remote work will be different, the following tips can help you add some structure to your day and avoid the pitfalls of nearly unlimited freedom.

Tip #1: Use the morning hours wisely
Since you no longer have a commute, the morning hours can be a great opportunity to get work done. Productivity experts recommend that you wake up the same time you normally would if you were going into the office, but we recommend waking up literally

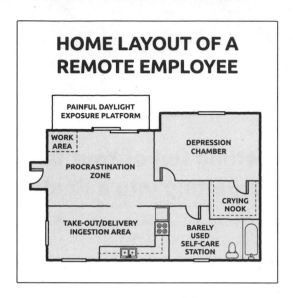

thirty seconds before your manager starts checking to see if you're online.

Tip #2: Create a dedicated workspace

To create more structure, it's important to have a dedicated workspace. This allows you to separate your professional life from your personal, so whenever you're at your workstation, you can focus exclusively on work and not on the fact that your personal life is in shambles.

Tip #3: Minimize distractions

Many people find that when they work from home, there are more distractions than they expected. The dishes need to be done, the trash needs to be taken out, and the German national tied up in the basement won't stop screaming. Limit distractions by getting household chores done before sitting down to work, or after you've finished for the evening, and ask the people you live with to be mindful of the fact that even though you're at home, you're technically still at work.

Tip #4: Maintain a consistent schedule

Although working from home might feel a bit like early retirement, it's important to maintain a regular work schedule so that you don't underdo or overdo it. Starting and stopping work at the same time everyday ensures consistency and creates a healthy balance between your personal and professional lives, both of which involve sitting on the couch for hours and vacantly staring at a screen.

Tip #5: Take breaks throughout the day

It's easy to take breaks when you're in the office. But at home, it becomes more complicated since there's not much separation between you and your couch, your kitchen, and the counterfeit designer purse ring you're running out of your spare bedroom. Make sure to schedule breaks throughout the day, or you risk unnecessary burnout.

Tip #6: Make sure to leave the house

Since you no longer have to go into an office, you might find that you're spending an inordinate amount of time at home. This is why it's so important to leave the house, whether it's going out for a walk, working at a local coffee shop, or flying out to Vegas to audition for an experiential circus troupe. The key is to avoid letting yourself get cooped up at home.

PRODUCTIVITY HACKS

Staying productive is difficult enough but even more difficult when your dog has been staring at you from across the room for three hours straight. Here are some hacks to help maintain your productivity:

- Avoid multitasking.
- Work in short, timed bursts.
- Use website blockers to block distracting websites and apps.

- Secretly bring on an intern to do all of your work for you.
- Get rid of small distractions by asking your roommate to move out immediately.
- Constantly tell everyone you're "swamped" to avoid being assigned new tasks.
- Use wide margins to make it look like you've done more work.
- Identify your most difficult task and try to get somebody else to do it.

BENEFITS OF REMOTE WORK

The benefits of remote work are many. In addition to no longer having a commute, here are some upsides:

- financial savings
- more flexible schedule
- opportunity to simultaneously work another full-time job
- more opportunities to spy on neighbors
- flexibility to ignore supervisor's repeated messages and video calls
- more time to develop a dark and mysterious alter ego
- can eat a plastic container full of melted cheese for lunch without fear of judgment

NEGATIVE EFFECTS OF REMOTE WORK

Unfortunately, if you're not careful, working remotely can have some detrimental effects. Here are some things you'll want to avoid:

- working too many hours
- decreased productivity
- increased consumption of literally everything
- more opportunities for neighbors to spy on you
- increased risk of accidentally locking self in bathroom

- no valid excuse when spouse wants to spend more time together
- reduction in volume of oxygen left over for roommates

FINAL THOUGHTS

Like anything else, remote work has its upsides and downsides. While some people might thrive on being locked in their bedroom all day, others will long for the camaraderie and structure found in an office. And no matter which side of the spectrum you're on, you can rest assured that your opinion is probably wrong.

But if you do choose (or are forced into) remote work, the most important thing you can do is get into a routine that works for *you*. Because without a regular routine, you're likely to flail, stress yourself out, and put your job at risk. So clear out that bedroom corner, wipe the drool stains from that old desk, and set up your new workstation. You can Live, Laugh, Love after the workday is over.

Video Call Etiquette
and How to Make It Look Like
You've Been Working All Day

R emote work is made possible by millions of slippery underground tubes known collectively as the "internet." Video conferencing software, which uses these tubes, allows us to connect with our coworkers from the comfort of our homes yet somehow still doesn't diminish the physical discomfort that comes with talking to some of our more abrasive colleagues.

As with everything work related, however, video calls require you to maintain professional etiquette. By adhering to the rules, both spoken and unspoken, you can guarantee that your call will be a pleasant experience, just probably not for you.

PROPER VIDEO CALL ETIQUETTE

Whether you're new to the world of videoconferencing software or an experienced user, the following rules will help ensure you don't make any videoconferencing mistakes:

Rule #1: Always be on time
Just as with any in-person meeting, punctuality is a must on a previously scheduled video call. Don't think that you can sneak in late

without anybody noticing, because it's even more obvious when it's on video. If you *are* running late, however, make sure to message the video host and accuse them of trying to sabotage your career.

Rule #2: Unless you're speaking, keep your mic muted

There are a few reasons why you should always keep your microphone muted during a meeting, but the biggest one is the potential for any background noise to break through and interrupt the speaker. There are few things as mortifying as your coworkers overhearing your significant other ask if "your tum-tum is still hurty" during a weekly planning session, so make sure that microphone icon stays a solid red.

Rule #3: Wear appropriate attire (at least from the waist up)

Even though you're not in the office, it's important to remain professional in your dress as well as your behavior. While you likely don't have to dress to the nines (unless your company requires it), it might make sense to take off the "my love language is Shrek" shirt and put on a sweater.

Rule #4: Make sure your technology is working

No matter which videoconferencing software you're using, always test it before the meeting to make sure it's functioning properly on your device. If you're unable to log in, troubleshoot the software by mashing the keyboard with your palm and striking the screen repeatedly until the camera turns on.

Rule #5: Pay attention when somebody else is speaking

During video meetings, it's easy to get distracted by email notifications and websites that have nothing to do with work. Avoid this trap by closing out all of your tabs and focusing on the person speaking. The unfortunate irony to this, however, is that the more you focus, the longer the person is likely to keep talking.

Rule #6: Try not to stare at yourself

There's something strangely hypnotizing about seeing yourself on camera, especially in the live format of an active video call. But if you're in a meeting, avoid the urge to stare at your little square. Not only are other people likely to notice, but trust us when we say that nothing good can come from catching a real glimpse of your hairline.

Rule #7: Unless it's a lunch meeting, put the food away

Having a snack during an in-person meeting might be acceptable, but when the format changes to video, it's best to put the food away. In the event that the meeting is a working lunch or dinner, practice good dining etiquette: chew with your mouth closed, wipe your face, and always offer the person you're meeting with some of your meal.

THINGS YOU SHOULD NEVER DO ON A VIDEO CALL

In some cases, your video meetings might actually be recorded. For this reason (and many others), here are some things you should never do during a video call:

- Never take an important video call on your mobile device.
- Never walk (or drive) around while in a video meeting.
- Never livestream your meeting to the dark web.
- Never bad-mouth a coworker in a recorded video meeting.
- Never ignore a meeting invite unless you have something way better to do that day.
- Never assume that what you say isn't being recorded, remixed into a dance song, and getting millions of monthly views on YouTube.

EYE POSITION DURING A VIDEO CALL

UP

I AM TRYING TO COME UP WITH
AN EXCUSE FOR WHY MY
ASSIGNMENT ISN'T DONE

DOWN

I CAN'T BELIEVE I SPILLED
ICED COFFEE ALL
OVER MY LAP AGAIN

LEFT

I AM TRYING TO UPDATE
MY RÉSUMÉ ON MY
SECOND MONITOR

RIGHT

I CAN'T STOP
STARING AT MYSELF
IN DISGUST

STRAIGHT AHEAD

I AM FOCUSED, COMMITTED,
AND TAKING PRESCRIPTION
MEDICATION

HOW TO MAKE IT LOOK LIKE YOU'VE BEEN WORKING ALL DAY

As we mentioned before, the freedom of remote work can lead to procrastination, a fact of which management is well aware. So if you've spent the day doomscrolling instead of working and you need to hop on a video call, here's how to make it look like you've been hard at work:

- Stack a handful of work-related nonfiction books directly behind you.
- Make sure you're holding a pen.
- Mess up your hair so it looks like you've been too busy for self-care.
- Occasionally rub your temples in a clockwise circular motion.
- Set your alarm to go off every few minutes so it looks like you have a packed schedule.
- Constantly check your watch while occasionally shaking your head.

- Place a full meal on your desk so that it looks like you haven't had time to eat.

FINAL THOUGHTS

There's no doubt that video calls have changed the workplace. No longer do we have to sit in a stuffy conference room and get screamed at. Instead, we can get screamed at from the comfort of home. In this brave new world, convenience is everything.

But convenience comes at a cost, and that cost is the risk of doing something wildly embarrassing as every single one of your coworkers sits there watching, judging, recording, and emailing a *New York Times* reporter. So make use of new tech, but do it carefully. Otherwise, you might wish you were back in the office.

When Pets Become Coworkers and Refuse to Follow the Rules

Many of us have pets: strange animals that cohabitate our space without cooking, cleaning, or paying rent. Pets are a great source of joy for the overworked masses, bringing laughter, stress relief, and hair. Lots and lots of hair.

But when you suddenly find yourself working from home, your relationship with your pets might change, and not always for the better. In some cases, your companion might welcome all the time you're spending with them. But in others, they might feel like you're intruding on their personal space. In either case, you're faced with an uncomfortable truth: your pet has now become your coworker.

HOW TO PREPARE YOUR PETS FOR REMOTE WORK

Your newfound time at home might come as a shock to your furry companions, which is why it's important to prepare them for this sudden change in lifestyle. Here are some tips to help your pets adjust:

- Schedule a house meeting to discuss your new work arrangements. Depending on how smart your pets are, they may or may not understand what's happening.

- Practice keeping your door closed to minimize distractions when working. The pets belong *outside* the door.
- Make sure you train your pets not to distract you during a video call. If possible, train them to pretend they're sick on command so you can take time off to "bring them to the vet."
- Since you will certainly be overfeeding yourself while working from home, try not to overfeed your pet.
- Walk and exercise your pets regularly. It wouldn't kill you to join them once in a while too.

HOW TO PREPARE YOUR PETS FOR A RETURN TO THE OFFICE

While working remotely can create some human–pet conflict, a return to the office after a prolonged period of remote work can also have detrimental effects on your pet's psyche. Here are some tips to prepare them for those days when you need to head to the office in person:

- Incorporate short departures into your workday so your pets can adjust to your absence. Do the same with your coworkers.
- Try not to fawn over your pet before leaving as this can increase their anxiety. Just because you're freaking out about going into the office doesn't mean everybody else has to.
- Leave something for your pet to focus on while you're gone, such as a chew toy or the presentation that's due Friday that you haven't even started.
- It's possible that your pet might be destructive after being left alone for the first time. Don't be angry with them—after all, it's not their fault you lack the skills, talent, and charisma to land a better job.

PETS AS COWORKERS: OFFICIAL POWER RANKINGS

DOG (97)
- **+** WILL INCREASE YOUR POPULARITY AMONG HUMAN COWORKERS
- **−** SPORADIC BARKING DURING CALLS

FISH (84)
- **+** GREAT LISTENERS
- **−** MIGHT BE DEAD FOR A FEW DAYS BEFORE YOU NOTICE

CAT (75)
- **+** INDEPENDENT, LOW MAINTENANCE, KEEP TO THEMSELVES
- **−** TYPICALLY NOT TEAM PLAYERS

SLOTH (67)
- **+** SLOW, STEADY, AND METICULOUS
- **−** NOTORIOUS FOR MISSING DEADLINES

SNAKE (62)
- **+** FITS IN WELL WITH MOST COWORKERS
- **−** HAS TENDENCY TO CONSTRICT AND SWALLOW COMPUTER MOUSE

HAMSTER (55)
- **+** HIGH ENERGY, ENTHUSIASTIC
- **−** CONSTANTLY SPINNING THEIR WHEELS BUT GETTING NOTHING DONE

BRINGING PETS INTO THE OFFICE

Some companies will allow you to bring your pet into the office. While this can be a great perk, it's important to make sure your pet can handle it and to take the steps necessary so that everything goes smoothly. Here are some tips for those who want to bring their pet to work:

- Let your team know ahead of time that you'll be bringing your pet. This is a common courtesy and will give your coworkers time to prepare to talk in that annoying high-pitched voice.
- Pack all the necessities your pet will need throughout the day: food and water dishes, treats, toys, a bed, poop disposal bags, and Xanax. (The Xanax is for you.)
- Make sure to animal-proof your work area. Ask coworkers to pick up anything off the floor they wouldn't want an animal to touch. Make sure you explain that it's literally an animal and not just somebody from sales.

- Keep an eye on your pet. Don't allow your pet to wander around unattended, as there's a chance your manager will hire it and not pay it what it's worth.

FINAL THOUGHTS

Despite the strange smells they emit, pets can give our life meaning, and for many people, they're just like family members. And since our pets are essentially relatives, why shouldn't they get to experience the drudgery of the workplace too?

So, whether you work from home while your pet loudly licks themselves next to you or bring your pet with you to the office so they can understand why you cry yourself to sleep every night, you should always appreciate having a pet as a coworker. At a minimum, you can be sure that it's better than working with another human being.

Cabin Fever: How to WFH Without Losing Your Mind

During the Klondike Gold Rush of the late nineteenth century, enterprising prospectors trekked through Alaska to the Yukon in search of riches. To survive the harsh winters, some would stay in cabins, where the lack of daylight and prolonged isolation caused them to lose their minds.

The modern-day employee has much in common with these prospectors, starting with the fact that neither one will ever be rich. Similarly, the prolonged isolation of remote work can cause problems, which is why it's important to be mindful of your mental health when working from home.

HOW TO AVOID REMOTE WORK BURNOUT

Here are some steps you can take to avoid going off the deep end while working from home:

Step 1: Take a shower and change clothes

It might be tempting to roll out of bed and start working in your pajamas, but taking a shower and changing clothes every morning can have a therapeutic effect and add structure to your day. If you've forgotten how to shower, there are some explainer videos available on YouTube.

Step 2: Schedule time to exercise

Whether it's a walk around the block or an hour of high-intensity cardio, you should try to incorporate exercise into your workday. Exercise has been shown to reduce stress, help your immune system, and get you in shape so you can defeat your manager in physical combat.

Step 3: Put on some music or a podcast

Spending the day in silence can take a toll, so it can be helpful to throw on some music or a podcast for background noise. Another option is to have a conversation with your coworkers or boss, which can be quite—actually, on second thought, just do the podcast thing.

Step 4: Stay off social media

While it might be tempting to spend the day scrolling through your frenemies' inane postings on Facebook or Instagram, it won't do much to ease your anxiety. In fact, studies have linked prolonged social media use to an increase in loneliness, anxiety, and wondering how the hell Bryce Gibbons from high school became a doctor. (That guy was a complete moron!)

Step 5: Try to maintain a healthy diet

Freedom, loneliness, and boredom can all lead to overeating and other unhealthy food habits. To avoid these pitfalls, try to stick to a healthy and well-balanced diet. Or at least stick to telling people you're sticking to a healthy and well-balanced diet while eating whatever you want.

Step 6: Make sure to set boundaries with your boss and coworkers

Remote work can make it feel like you should always be available, no matter the hour. That's why you should set boundaries with coworkers and let them know that after a certain time (10:00 a.m.

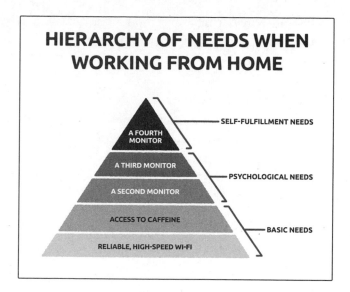

is too early), any questions or requests will have to wait until the following day.

Step 7: Take frequent breaks

To avoid burnout, you should schedule frequent breaks throughout the day. These breaks allow you to decompress, recharge, come up with better excuses for your professional failures, and improve performance.

Step 8: Make the most of your days off

Since you're working from home, it's important to switch things up on your days off. If possible, leave the house and try to structure your day so that it's different from your normal routine, which consists of dissociatively staring into space while waiting for a chronically underpaid driver to deliver your fast food.

Step 9: Don't rely on artificial remedies

While caffeine, sugar, and high-calorie foods can give us a temporary boost, the downsides are usually worse than the upsides. For this reason, you shouldn't rely on temporary artificial boosters as a crutch and should instead get an actual prescription for something more powerful.

Step 10: Stay in contact with others

Unfortunately, the best way to counter prolonged isolation is by staying in touch with people, whether in person, through a video chat, or with a simple phone call. So put away the remote control and call that old friend from college; even though it will be torturous at first, it'll probably help.

WHAT TO DO IF YOU'VE LOST YOUR MIND

Despite your best efforts, there's a good chance you might still lose your mind when working from home. If this happens, don't worry, it's perfectly normal, and there are ways to use it to your advantage. Here's what to do if you've accidentally lost your mind:

- Contact your supervisor and let them know you've definitely gone off the deep end.
- If they're skeptical, send an example of your most recent work (which is likely to be complete gibberish) for proof.
- Take time off so you can get back to normal, then take another few months off after that.
- Try to monetize your newfound madness by selling paintings on Etsy.
- If it's an option, consider going back into the office.
- Develop and sell a course called "How to Avoid Losing Your Mind," making yourself a small fortune.

FINAL THOUGHTS

Humans are social creatures, and many simply can't handle spending their days alone, staring at a computer screen while the crushing weight of existence bears down on them like a rockslide. This is why it's so important to take care of ourselves both physically and mentally, no matter how much labor your employer demands.

If you ever find yourself getting overwhelmed, try to remember that it's just a job, and there are way more important things in life. After all, what's the worst that could happen? That you could get fired, become unable to pay your bills, end up on the streets, and die a horrible death? Yeah, that . . . actually *does* sound pretty bad, doesn't it?

Proper Dress Code
When Working Remotely

I f you resent having to dress up for work every morning, then you might find the flexibility of being able to wear (or not wear) whatever you want quite liberating. One of the unspoken benefits of remote work is the ability to spend the day wrapped in an adult-sized onesie without the prying, judgmental eyes of your coworkers.

But don't let your newfound fashion freedom fool you, because there are plenty of clothing considerations to take into account when working from home. Let's review the proper dress code.

PROPER WFH DRESS CODE

For the most part, unless you're required to attend a video meeting, you're free to wear what you want. Here are some ideas:

- a comfortable sweater or sweatshirt
- sweatpants or flexible jeans
- a soft, cozy button-up shirt
- a blanket draped over your shoulders like a medieval cloak
- a formal evening gown in an effort to relive the best night of your life
- a polo shirt with your company's logo crossed out with a black marker

PROPER VIDEO MEETING DRESS CODE

Video meetings usually require more professional attire. Here are some ideas on what to wear when the camera is on:

- a well-fitting shirt or sweater
- a blazer or suit and tie (depending on the formality of the meeting)
- a dress, skirt, or blouse
- a tuxedo T-shirt
- a crewneck sweatshirt with a picture of your thirteen-year-old pug on it
- accessories such as a light scarf, a headband, or a necklace with all your baby teeth glued to it

OTHER TIPS

- Since the camera will only pick up the upper half of your body, focus mostly on what you're wearing from the waist up.
- Try to avoid any overpowering colors or patterns; if your co-workers wanted to feel like they were on an acid trip, they'd just drink the artificial creamer in the break room.
- Wear a watch, as it can show that you're keeping track of time and not just rewatching *Game of Thrones* while waiting for your lawsuit settlement to come in.
- If you ever have questions about what is and isn't appropriate to wear, just ask your manager or human resources coordinator so they can fire you and get it over with.

NEW WFH FASHION STYLES

The rise of remote work has created new fashion categories that have replaced traditional trends in favor of more comfortable attire. Here are some of them:

- sporty recluse
- stretchy sweatpants chic
- living room couture
- giant disposable bib (this is just a giant disposable bib)
- activewear for the inactive
- lock-yourself-in-the-bedroom bohemian

FINAL THOUGHTS

Working from home certainly does give you more flexibility when it comes to your chosen attire, but as long as your income is dependent on the whims of people you would never have anything to do with in real life, you can never truly let your fashion flag fly.

However, it's not all bad (just mostly bad). Avoiding the office does allow you to lounge around in sweats all day as long as the internet connection remains stable. But if your manager wants you on a video call, then you better suit up because, at its core, the workplace is all about judgment—constant, inescapable judgment.

PART 5

Meetings
(Whose Foot Is That?)

The most important, complex, and emotionally fraught event in the workplace usually takes the form of a meeting, defined as "an assembly of people, especially the members of a society or committee, for discussion or entertainment." The only entertainment you can expect in a workplace meeting, however, is the possibility that two of your coworkers will get into a juicy screaming match in front of everyone—a rare, but delightful sight.

Love them or hate them, meetings happen in every workplace, and every type of employee, no matter how junior, will be forced, at some point, to attend one. Some meetings will be short, and some will feel like they're never going to end; some will be enjoyable, and some will feel like a police interrogation. But whether the meeting is a productive one or not, you can always be sure that there's no way you'll ever walk out of a meeting and say, "Man, I'd really like to do *that* again."

In the following chapters, we'll dissect workplace meetings piece by piece and provide you with some tips and tricks to make the most of any meetings you might be unlucky enough to attend. There are many ways to ensure that meetings go smoothly, and as long as you follow our advice, and have an exit strategy coupled with a ready-made excuse, you'll easily survive any meeting that gets thrown your way.

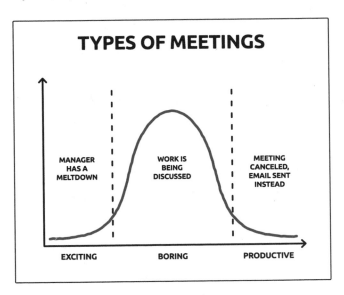

The Different Types of Meetings

In some ways, workplace meetings are all the same: a handful of (or at least two) ambivalent people are stuffed inside a room and forced to discuss things they get paid to pretend to care about until one of them finally puts an end to the charade and wraps things up. But in other ways, each meeting is unique, depending on its purpose, participants, level of importance, and whether or not there's an angry manager involved (though these meetings can be strangely exhilarating).

It's important to understand the different types of meetings, because knowledge is power (a good example of something you can say during a meeting to make it look like you're contributing), and because whether you want to or not, sooner or later, you're likely to find yourself sitting in a meeting, wondering where it all went wrong. So put on your most professional smile and try your best not to fall asleep, because if you want to get your next paycheck, you'll have to get used to your coworkers droning on and on about God knows what—that's what meetings are for.

Most meetings fall into one or more categories. Here are the most common ones:

The One-on-One

For anyone who loves awkward moments, the one-on-one meeting is second to none. This type of meeting consists of two people, usually a supervisor and their direct report, though equal coworkers might also meet to discuss a collaborative project. The upside to this type of meeting is that you can threaten the other participants without worrying about witnesses. The downside is they can threaten you without worrying about witnesses too. One-on-one meetings are perfect for discussing sensitive issues such as problems with your work (if meeting with your supervisor) or for planning a management coup (if meeting with colleagues). However, if you're ever invited to a one-on-one with your supervisor, be prepared for the worst.

The Full House

This type of meeting occurs when all members of a division or an entire company are packed like sardines into a conference room or function hall. Usually, the full house is organized in order to announce major events, changes, or as a quarterly or annual kickoff. The full-house meeting is easy enough to get through, as you're unlikely to be singled out among the crowd. On the flip side, these meetings can stretch for hours, or even an entire day, so it might take some stamina (or those glasses with the fake googly eyes on them) to survive without falling asleep.

The Pressure Cooker

The pressure cooker is possibly the most challenging type of meeting. During a pressure cooker, a sensitive subject is usually being discussed as everyone except the speaker sits silently, sometimes looking down at their feet to avoid eye contact. Sometimes the entire team is being chewed out; other times, a coworker is being reprimanded. In some rare cases, the meeting has been called because someone keeps drawing a picture of a nude SpongeBob on the marketing whiteboard. Any meeting can turn into a pressure cooker, given the right circumstances. All that's needed is tension, discomfort, awkward silence, and despair.

The Leaky Bucket

This type of meeting can barely be described as a meeting at all. The leaky bucket is a type of meeting where people come in and out of the room constantly, disrupting everybody involved and making it nearly impossible to focus or get anything done. Sometimes, people will get up and leave one by one. Other times, an entire contingent of participants will show up late or leave early. The only thing certain about the leaky bucket is that it will be unproductive—which, let's be honest, makes it better than the alternative.

The Pointless

To some degree, all meetings are pointless, as our impending doom cannot be arrested nor fully masked by the trivial distractions we use to take our mind off the inevitable. But there's pointless, and then there's *pointless*. This type of meeting is the latter, a complete waste of time for everyone involved. These meetings might start off promisingly enough: an agenda, good attendance, and the best intentions. But, usually within minutes, they devolve into meandering discussions that have nothing to do with the subject at hand and never recover. The pointless meeting is nice if you want to avoid work (hell yeah!), but it's also time you'll never get back, for better or worse.

The Productive

The rarest of them all, the productive meeting happens when everyone is focused, engaged, and firing on all cylinders—basically when everyone is on Adderall. This doesn't happen very often because most workers spend their days struggling against the myriad of distractions that make contemporary life a postapocalyptic hellscape. But when it does, you can feel the energy. And if you ever find yourself attending a meeting that becomes productive, make sure you pull your weight—because in this type of meeting, everyone has to contribute.

The Feast

During this type of meeting, you will get to eat free food. But the downside is that it's usually been scheduled at the point in the day when you're at your absolute hungriest, which means you won't be able to focus on anything except for the plastic tray of lukewarm Panera Bread sandwiches sitting idly on the conference room table, taunting you and your rumbling stomach like a desert mirage. The upside, of course, is the opportunity to eat for free. But unless you had the foresight to grab a snack beforehand, this type of meeting won't be very pleasant for you until you get your grubby hands on that mediocre food.

The D. B. Cooper

The D. B. Cooper is named after the famous skyjacker, still the only airline hijacker who's never been caught. This type of meeting occurs when someone hijacks the meeting and never relinquishes control. Usually, it's the office blowhard launching into a long-winded explanation about why something should be done the way *they* think it should. No amount of overt social queues, polite interruptions, or attempts to change the conversation can put a stop to their insufferable rant. You can try all you want, but once the meeting has been hijacked—just like D. B. Cooper did—you'll never get it back.

The Brainstormer

Meetings arranged for the specific purpose of coming up with new ideas are called brainstormers, and you can bet your bottom dollar that the ideas these meetings produce will range from the comical to the patently absurd. To be sure, decent ideas will occasionally be voiced, but they'll quickly fall to the wayside in favor of the dumbest, most ludicrous schemes ever known to man. If you're ever invited to a brainstormer, make sure to write down your best ideas. Then take the piece of paper, crumple it up, and throw it in the trash. Good ideas are *not* welcome here—only preposterous ones.

FINAL THOUGHTS

Meetings come in all shapes and sizes and can cause varying degrees of embarrassment. Whether it's a quick one-on-one with your thrice-divorced manager, or a mind-numbing barn burner discussing which shade of magenta to use on that font no one will ever actually see, meetings can help you accomplish anything except the things that actually matter.

That's not to say they're not important. Quite the contrary, meetings help add structure to our day, give us something to not look forward to, and bring the team together in a room where they can more easily infect each other with airborne illnesses. If, however, you feel an overwhelming sense of dread after receiving that meeting invite, the following chapter might help.

Excuses to Get Out of Meetings While Making People Feel Bad for You

If you've ever wished that you could snap your fingers and make every meeting on your calendar disappear, you're not alone. Impending meetings have led to many sleepless nights, not to mention a myriad of creative excuses to get out of attending. While a handful of these excuses have likely been legitimate, the overwhelming majority of them are contrived and, unfortunately, a bit difficult to believe.

Anything worth doing is worth doing well, and that includes lying. If you're going to tell tall tales to get out of a meeting, then put in some effort and make them actually sound believable. If you don't, then you risk becoming known as the person who lies to get out of meetings, instead of the person who blacked out at the company party and tried to fight the valet.

GOOD EXCUSES TO GET OUT OF A MEETING

If you're looking for a good (and believable) excuse, try using one of the following:

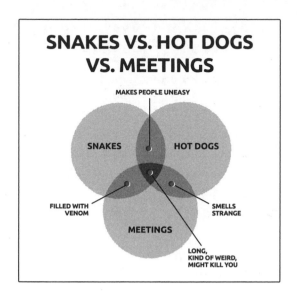

- "I'm sorry, but I'm not feeling well and can't make it to the meeting."
- "Unfortunately, I had a family emergency and won't be able to attend."
- "You'll have to excuse my absence, since I will be praying for forgiveness during that time."
- "There's no way I can make it to the meeting; I'm way too tired from applying to other jobs."
- "I really wanted to go to this meeting, but I actually had it mixed up with my celibacy support group."
- "Unfortunately, I can't make it due to a conflict. The conflict is between the meeting and my desire not to go."
- "This meeting sounds incredibly interesting . . . just not to me."
- "Something important (the McRib is back!) has just come up, which means I won't be able to attend the meeting."
- "Would it be possible to reschedule our meeting? I can't make it due to who I am as a person."

HOW TO GAIN SYMPATHY FROM
YOUR COWORKERS

Sympathy, like any other emotion, should be wielded strategically, like an ice axe during a fight to the death while on a mountain climb. Using sympathy the right way will not only help you get out of meetings and the other bare-minimum responsibilities of your job, it will also lay the groundwork for better treatment from your coworkers. Simply put: the more colleagues see you as a victim, the more you can get away with. Keeping that in mind, here are some tips to help you gain sympathy from your coworkers:

1. Find (or make up) a sympathetic family member

There's nothing that earns sympathy quite like made-up stories about family members, whether it's a dying uncle, a troubled child, or a spouse who is struggling with having been run over by a train. Don't be afraid to embellish the facts, as truth is usually stranger than fiction. And if you don't have any problematic family members, just make one up. *Pro tip:* sprinkle some truth into every story to make it more believable.

2. Apologize

When telling stories to gain sympathy, always apologize for burdening the listener with your "reality." Similarly, try saying things like, "This couldn't have come at a worse time," and "I really hope this doesn't get in the way of this project," showing that you're concerned about the job. Not only will this help you sound more convincing—it will also turn you into a more sympathetic character.

3. Use body language

Using the right body language can be a great way to earn sympathy. Practice doing things like sighing and shaking your head or putting your elbows on the table and rubbing your face with your hands. When someone inevitably asks you what's wrong, just tell them you have "a lot going on," but that you'll "probably be okay." Most people will get the message.

4. Don't overdo it
The most believable sob stories are ones that are subtle enough to be realistic, so make sure you don't use the plot of *Million Dollar Baby* to get out of having to go to work. In that same vein, a person who lays it on too thick or overdoes the melodrama risks irritating the very people they're trying to gain sympathy from. So, no audible crying, no excessive moping, and, for the love of God, no crowdfunding links.

5. Consume sad and depressing content in front of everyone
A great way to gain sympathy is to make sure that whatever you're watching, reading, or listening to is incredibly sad, reflecting your supposed pitiable state. Books are a great place to start, even if you don't like to read, because people will see them on your desk and assume the worst. Just go to the nearest bookstore, go into the nonfiction or self-help section, and find books that have been written to help people dealing with serious problems. *Pro tip:* if you want people to feel sorry for you, *do not* let them see you reading this book.

FINAL THOUGHTS

In life, we're often forced to do things we don't want to do. And at work, we're *always* forced to do things we don't want to do. Meetings are at the top of that list, which is why having a strategy for getting out of them is so important. If you don't plan ahead, you might end up getting stuck at the office until the accounting team starts their nightly incriminating document shredding routine— so make sure you've practiced your excuses.

Sympathy, meanwhile, can be an effective tool not only for getting out of meetings but for getting out of anything that causes you even the slightest bit of personal inconvenience. Companies are strategic, and employees should be too! So make sure you line up your excuses and plan your pity party well in advance. If you execute on both counts, you can spend your afternoons eating Oreos in bed like a degenerate, instead of sitting through another mindless presentation.

Camera Position:
How to Set Up Your Laptop
for Maximum Dominance

Video meetings are, unfortunately, here to stay. Whether you love them or hate them, approaching video meetings strategically can help maximize your standing among your coworkers, so if they ever decide to cross you, you'll be able to crush them and ensure that no one gets between you and your climb up the ranks of the corporate food chain (all the way up to the second or third rung from the bottom, if you're lucky to even get that far).

The video meeting, therefore, is not much different from an in-person rendezvous, especially in terms of its implications for office politics. So before you click that "Join Meeting" button and get transported into a virtual world filled with awkward silence, make sure to set yourself up so that you can leave the meeting knowing you did everything possible to make yourself look good.

HOW TO DOMINATE VIRTUAL MEETINGS

In order to come away from an interaction feeling like you've won, you have to make yourself look powerful while making everyone else look weak. The same goes for virtual meetings, where egos and personalities are (literally) on display. Here are some tips to help you dominate video meetings:

RECIPE: VIRTUAL MEETINGS

INGREDIENTS

1/2 CUP FLOUR

1 TSP BAKING SODA

1/2 CUP MARGARINE

1 CUP WHOLE MILK

2 EGGS

2 CUPS SUGAR

1/8 TSP NUTMEG

BAKE ON 375° FOR 30 TO 40 MINUTES OR UNTIL GOLDEN BROWN.

DIRECTIONS

STEP 1: KEEP GLASS FILLED WITH VODKA OUT OF CAMERA VIEW

STEP 2: MAKE SURE YOU'RE MUTED BEFORE CALLING KEVIN A BRIDGE TROLL

STEP 3: CLOSE ALL INCRIMINATING TABS BEFORE SHARING YOUR SCREEN

STEP 4: HIRE AN ACTOR TO PLAY THE SIGNIFICANT OTHER YOU'VE BEEN LYING ABOUT

STEP 5: NOD AND SAY "UH-HUH" TO MAKE IT LOOK LIKE YOU ARE CONTRIBUTING

STEP 6: SET YOUR ALARM TO GO OFF AT THE THIRTY-MINUTE MARK SO IT LOOKS LIKE YOU HAVE TO LEAVE

Tip #1: Sit close to the camera

If you sit too far away, you'll look small and diminutive and won't be able to intimidate people. Always sit close to the camera, so that everyone can feel your inescapable presence in the room with them. And if you really want to dominate the meeting, buy a high-quality camera that shows every single pore in your skin, increasing everyone's discomfort.

Tip #2: Set up the correct lighting

While most professionals recommend setting up a bright lamp for continuous lighting, this approach won't help you in your quest to mercilessly dominate the people you work with. Instead, turn the lights off and draw your shades, then buy a cheap flashlight and position it under your chin as if you're in *The Blair Witch Project*. This will make you look terrifying and ensure that your coworkers immediately fall in line.

Tip #3: Pick the right background

Sometimes, the right background can make all the difference. Some people prefer to use a bookshelf, while others prefer a blank wall to avoid distractions. If you want to overpower your coworkers, however, you should pick an intimidating background such as an unchecked inferno or the Fall of Constantinople. Backgrounds can help, so make sure to use them.

Tip #4: Focus on sound

Believe it or not, the type of microphone you use can have a major impact. If your computer microphone echoes a lot or doesn't pick up sound, it's worth investing in an accessory mic. Once you've got crystal-clear audio, you can add sound effects like a muffled scream or a ticking clock to make your coworkers nervous.

Tip #5: Dress the part

You can't just throw any old outfit on and expect to dominate the people you work with. Instead, take the time to do it right and put together the perfect fashion statement, one that screams "I'm sooo much better than you!" Some ideas: a cloak and a top hat, a suit made out of hundred-dollar bills, a shirt with your coworkers' crossed-out faces on it. Or, to show the utmost confidence, skip the clothes altogether—that'll really make a statement.

Tip #6: Posture matters

If you slouch your way through your meetings, you can hardly expect anybody to fear you. Be mindful of your posture, keeping your back perfectly straight and your chin raised as if you've just discovered you're part of the aristocracy. When speaking, pull your shoulders back and puff out your chest like a rooster, and don't be afraid to stand up, so that you can literally *and* figuratively look down on the people you work with.

Tip #7: Speak confidently

The way you speak can have a massive impact on how people perceive you. You can come off as confident and domineering, or you can come off as a timid pushover—the choice is yours. The trick to projecting confidence is to speak clearly, to project your voice, and to stand by what you say, even if you're proven wrong using logic and facts. By doubling down on your incorrect statements, you will show coworkers that you won't be cowed into submission; that way, the next time they think about correcting you, they'll think twice.

Tip #8: Interrupt whenever possible

Letting other people speak is polite. But you're not trying to be polite—you're trying to dominate. So make sure to cut people off midsentence, especially when they're taking forever to get to the point. Even though some coworkers might find it frustrating that you refuse to let them get a word in edgewise, this is a small price to pay to show everybody that you're in charge and that you'll talk whenever you feel like it, no matter what.

FINAL THOUGHTS

Remember, just because you're working from home doesn't mean you can't jockey for power and status. Video meetings are a great place to showcase your dominance, and you can bet that your coworkers won't soon forget your willingness to step all over them for your own personal gain.

And if the people you work with refuse to fall in line, don't give up hope. There will be plenty of opportunities to show your coworkers that you won't give up your quest for absolute power anytime soon. Just because they've won the battle doesn't mean they'll win the war. Though, based on your prior history of seeing things through to completion, it's actually quite likely they'll win the war. Either way, give it your best shot!

How to Come Back Strong After You Spent the Entire Meeting on Twitter

We live in a distraction-filled world, and meetings (especially remote ones) can be so monotonous that we sometimes tune out and instinctively turn to the one thing in life that's never let us down: our phone. And although there's plenty of interesting stuff inside those nifty little contraptions, most of it—okay, all of it—has been designed to help us waste time rather than to help us become more productive employees (sounds awful) and better human beings (unlikely).

Most people, however, are unable to resist the magnetic pull of that beautifully illuminated screen, and once we've started scrolling, it'll take an earthquake or some other human tragedy to pull us back to the real world. But if you've accidentally spent an entire meeting having your self-esteem destroyed on social media, don't fret. You can still come back strong and make it look like you've been paying attention the entire time.

HOW TO STAY FOCUSED DURING MEETINGS

They say that a smart person knows how to get out of trouble, while a wise person knows how to avoid it to begin with. Since you're neither, this proverb doesn't really apply. But if you want to avoid embarrassing moments, it can help to steer clear of distractions. Here are some ways to stay focused during your meetings:

Tip #1: Get energized beforehand

Before entering the meeting, try doing an activity that increases your heart rate, so you can remain focused throughout. You can do things like listen to music, do some push-ups or jumping jacks, or download a copy of your credit report and calculate how much outstanding debt you have. As long as it gets the blood pumping, it's likely to help.

Tip #2: Fuel your body correctly

There's no question that what you eat can affect your focus and concentration. If you want to remain focused, stay away from fatty foods, which can make you lethargic. Instead, drink a bottle of wine on an empty stomach, which will keep your energy levels high throughout.

Tip #3: Take notes

Believe it or not, taking notes during a meeting can actually be a useful way to help you stay focused. Whether it's on a laptop or a pad and paper, notes can keep you engaged and help you retain key concepts. While you can't document the entire meeting, focus on the important stuff, like the speaker's personal appearance, your best guess about their salary, and whether you approve of their outfit. These are the things that matter.

Tip #4: Be an active participant

It's much easier to lose yourself to distraction when you're not actively taking part in a meeting, so make it a point to get involved. The best way to do this is by asking questions, and the best questions to ask are intensely personal ones. If you're able to muster up the courage to ask someone whether they find you attractive, you can bet that you (along with everyone else) will be laser-focused on the answer (no).

Tip #5: Put away your phone

When it comes to avoiding distractions, this is the best piece of advice you can possibly take. Putting your phone out of reach will eliminate your ability to pick it up and start scrolling. The reality, however, is that you're never going to do any of these things, so let's all save each other the trouble and move onto how you can make it look like you've been paying attention the whole time.

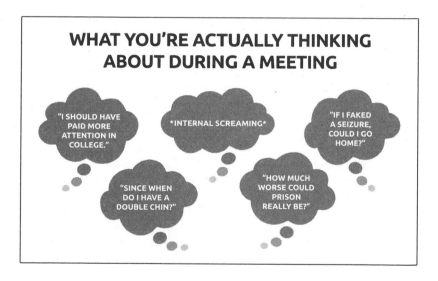

WHAT YOU'RE ACTUALLY THINKING ABOUT DURING A MEETING

"I SHOULD HAVE PAID MORE ATTENTION IN COLLEGE."

INTERNAL SCREAMING

"IF I FAKED A SEIZURE, COULD I GO HOME?"

"SINCE WHEN DO I HAVE A DOUBLE CHIN?"

"HOW MUCH WORSE COULD PRISON REALLY BE?"

HOW TO MAKE IT LOOK LIKE YOU'VE BEEN PAYING ATTENTION

The key to being a successful meeting participant is to make it look like you've been paying attention (rather than thinking about cheese) the entire time the presenters were speaking. Here are some tips and tricks that can help you pull it off:

Tip #1: Use your body language

Your body is a temple, but it's also a useful tool for workplace deception. When participating in a meeting, turn your body so that it faces whoever is speaking and nod along every now and then to show you're engaged and not just picturing the military tribunals you'd stage for your enemies if you were ever elected president.

Tip #2: Make sure to remember an important word or two

To make it look like you've been paying attention, you don't need to remember everything that's being discussed; you need to remember only a key word or concept. By being able to recite a word or two from the meeting, you'll make it a lot more difficult for any accusations that you haven't been paying attention to be taken seriously. Muddy the waters whenever possible. It will help.

Tip #3: Speak up

You might think that it's risky to speak up when you have no clue about the topic of discussion, but, in fact, the opposite is true. The trick is to make statements that can apply to anything, such as, "Let's make sure we're all in alignment first," or "What's the long-term play here?" By making general statements, you can come off as a team player without committing yourself to an auditable position—so speak up and then go right back to relaxing.

FINAL THOUGHTS

As you read through the last section, you might have thought to yourself: "Wouldn't it be easier just to pay attention rather than going through all the trouble to pretend?" The answer is no, it would not be easier. Because most meetings (with the exception of highly dramatic ones) are mind-numbingly boring, requiring an inordinate amount of self-discipline and personal effort to stay awake, let alone focused. For this reason, it's much easier to zone out and let the chips fall where they may—the alternative is just too demanding.

But don't feel bad, because you're not the only one who has a hard time paying attention. And let's be honest: this won't be the first or last time you have to pretend in order to keep your job. Pretending is one of the most important skills you can learn if you want to advance in corporate America. So, rather than getting an advanced degree or learning a trade, in the long run you'd be much better off taking some acting classes. Because if you can't convincingly fool your boss and your coworkers, the workplace is not the place for you.

Punting the Ball: How to Minimize the Chances of Getting More Work Assigned to You During a Meeting

The biggest risk of attending a meeting isn't losing precious work hours or being outed as a fraud; it's walking away from the meeting with more work. Meetings operate in such a way that, one minute, you might be nodding along in agreement with a new initiative, and the next, you've just been handed a demanding project with a hard deadline (basically, the kiss of death).

It's for this reason that you need to go into every meeting with a plan for how to avoid, or at least mitigate, additional assignments. Without a concrete plan, you risk leaving the size of your workload to chance, and hope, as they say, is never a strategy, especially in the workplace where all hope goes to die. So, before you go into that meeting, make sure to plan ahead—not by preparing for the meeting itself but by coming up with the right excuses for why you can't take on any more work. You'll certainly be glad you did.

If you want to continue your life of leisure, you need to avoid new assignments the same way you avoid the gym. Here are some tips:

Tip #1: Constantly talk about how "swamped" you are
To avoid having to do more work, it's important to look like you're

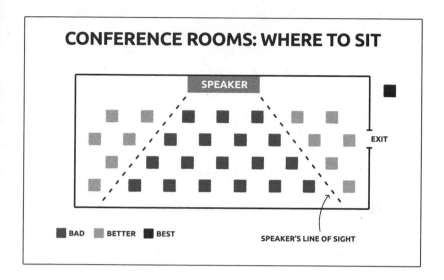

overwhelmed by the work you already have. The best way to do this is to repeatedly talk about how much you have on your plate, preferably within earshot of your manager (without saying it directly to them). This will ensure some hesitation on the part of whoever is responsible for assigning more work, making it more likely that it's assigned to a humbler (and hardworking) person.

Tip #2: Try to look as flustered as possible
Appearances are everything, and if you want to be the last person others look to in order to get stuff done, make sure to appear as if you're up to your eyeballs in work at all times. The best way to do this is to walk quickly everywhere you go as if you're always running late and to carry a stack of papers, preferably in a manila folder, which can add credibility to your claims of being overworked. When in doubt, just look busy.

Tip #3: Be proactive about deflecting assignments
Reacting to new demands is a lot more difficult than planning ahead. Whenever a new initiative comes up, have enough foresight

to suggest that a coworker will be the perfect person to take it on, framing it in a complimentary way so that it looks like you're elevating your coworker rather than avoiding the work. Say things like, "You know, this would be perfect for X," or "X is really good at this kind of stuff." By doing this, you'll get ahead of the problem, instead of waiting for it to become one.

Tip #4: Volunteer

It might sound counterintuitive, but by volunteering for more work, you can actually gain *more* control over what's being assigned. The key to doing this effectively is to be the first to volunteer and to pick only small aspects of the assignment, preferably the easiest ones. This will allow you to look like you're eager to contribute but will help you regain control. When volunteering, make sure to frame your limited efforts in terms of time constraints, explaining that you can take on X, because that's the only thing you'll have time to do.

Tip #5: Lie

Lying doesn't just come in handy when you're trying to land a job; it can also help you avoid getting swamped with further assignments. Whenever someone in a meeting suggests you take on more work, just come up with the most compelling lie about why you can't accept. To be sure, this will require you to think on your feet, which is why it's important to have a few lies prepared beforehand. Effective lies usually involve your health (and the health of your loved ones), allusions to being incredibly stressed out, and nebulous "personal issues," which are always a sure bet.

Tip #6: Disappear

This approach is most likely to work when new tasks are being assigned during a meeting. By disappearing, or simply not showing up, you reduce the likelihood of being burdened with more responsibilities, since some managers are reluctant to assign a project to someone who isn't there to go over the details. This tactic, however, can also backfire, as there's a possibility that you might be assigned a project in absentia, given the fact that you won't be there to defend yourself against more work. So be mindful of the risks when taking this approach—you might come to regret it.

FINAL THOUGHTS

Figuring out a way to get out of doing work is an art form; so, in some ways, you can consider yourself an artist. And, like most artists, you will likely spend the majority of your life being miserable before dying broke and alone, your spirit having been crushed by the weight of the world and all its demands, which will start long before the workplace, though there's no doubt the latter will certainly accelerate the process.

Fear not, however, because those who've mastered work avoidance can get more fulfillment from their jobs than those who take it in stride. After all, isn't this (avoiding responsibility) the hallmark of a fulfilling life? So, whether you choose to dodge, prevaricate, or half-ass it, make sure you give it your all (the avoidance, not the work itself), because the alternative asks way too much of you. And who needs all that stress anyway, right?

Ending Meetings:
The Cringey Last Goodbye

If the idea of being forced to attend a meeting sends a chill up your spine, then wrapping one up should flood you with an awesome wave of relief. There's something strangely gratifying about being set free after spending an hour or more discussing whatever minutiae your leadership is focused on that particular week. And, as an added bonus, everybody knows that the hour after a meeting is typically used to decompress, so there's little expectation that you'll actually get anything done—a small reprieve from the office's daily demands.

But before you get to bask in the sweet catharsis that is a meeting wrapped up, you'll have to get through it, or, better yet, figure out a way to bring about the end of said meeting early, not always an easy feat. But where there's a will, there's a way, and if you're strategic about it, you can proactively gain your freedom. And how can anyone expect people to do any actual work after they've spent the previous few hours trapped in meeting hell?

SIGNS THAT A MEETING CAN BE BROUGHT TO A CLOSE

Unfortunately, it's nearly impossible to end a meeting that's heated up. Only meetings that are showing fissures can be brought to a close. That's why, before attempting to shut things down, you need to look for signs that a meeting is faltering. Here are a few:

- There are long periods of uncomfortable silence (not unlike your dates).
- Everybody keeps checking their phones instead of paying attention.
- Paul from accounting has once again burst into tears.
- The window washers are making that annoying squeaking sound right outside the conference room.
- Anne Richardson has just confessed to embezzling company funds.
- Participants from the meeting scheduled after yours have filed into the room and are standing around impatiently checking their watches and tapping their toes.

HOW TO END A MEETING EARLY

To end a meeting early, you need to be strategic. Here are some tips:

Tip #1: Start clearing your throat

While clearing your throat on its own won't end a meeting, it will help get the wheels turning and plant the idea into people's heads. Start off with a small throat clearing, then ramp things up, clearing it every thirty seconds, then every ten seconds, then, finally, nonstop throat clearing. If your coworkers don't get the hint, just raise the volume.

Tip #2: Set a timer

It can be helpful to set a timer in order to keep a meeting running on schedule. If you want to end the meeting earlier, however, you'll have to find a way to shorten the end time without anyone noticing. This can be tricky to pull off, but if you can distract everyone with a false accusation against a coworker, you might be able to do it without being noticed.

Tip #3: Make everyone extremely uncomfortable

There's no quicker way to get everybody out of a meeting than by making things extremely awkward and uncomfortable. Most people can't stand embarrassing situations, so the more disconcerting you can make things, the better. You can do this by bringing up highly personal issues or by simply putting your face in your hands and refusing to acknowledge anyone when they ask you what's wrong. If you really commit to it, the meeting will be over in no time.

Tip #4: Pull the fire alarm

This option should only be considered as a last resort, since there are potential legal repercussions you might face if you're caught. However, if you want a guarantee that a meeting will end ahead of schedule, there's no better choice than pulling the fire alarm. To avoid detection, make sure to pull an alarm that's somewhat out of sight, perhaps the one normally found in the staircase. And always check for cameras, because the last thing you want to do is lose your job—wink, wink.

THE CRINGE-INDUCING GOODBYE

Whether you've pulled the rip cord and ended the meeting early or let it run its (unpleasant) natural course, the end of a meeting means that it's time to awkwardly say goodbye to your fellow participants, which, in many cases, can be more uncomfortable than that time your parents tried to talk to you about why you were taking so long in the bathroom.

But it doesn't have to be this way. When done correctly, saying goodbye can feel perfectly natural. Here's how to do it the right way:

- **Get ready.** Prepare for the end of the meeting by picking up everything you brought with you in order to avoid having to come back and doing the dreaded double goodbye.
- **Be direct.** There's no need to hem and haw before saying goodbye. Don't beat around the bush—just come out and say it, the same way you say all the other nonsense that comes into your head.
- **Look people in the eye.** This will be difficult for you since you have a guilty conscience (for good reason), but it's important to look people in the eye when saying goodbye—it's considered proper etiquette and should not be avoided.
- **Don't leave too early.** As much as you might want to run out of the room, make sure you've had a chance to say the proper

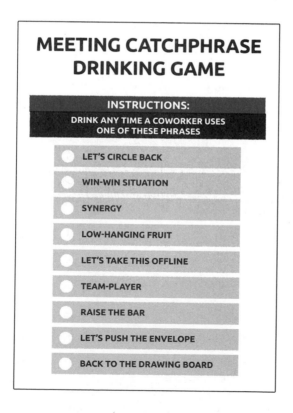

goodbyes. Otherwise, you might come off as someone who doesn't want to be part of the team, which, actually, is true.

- **If it's a video meeting, add a few seconds to account for delays.** Leaving a video meeting can be difficult, since you're forced to stare at each other for those few awkward moments before the camera finally shuts off. Similarly, make sure to wait a few seconds to account for delays; otherwise, you risk signing off in the middle of somebody saying goodbye—funny but rude.

FINAL THOUGHTS

If you've suffered through a long, tedious meeting, the last thing you want to do is prolong the misery a second longer than you have to. That's why knowing how to end meetings can be so valuable: it's never too early to get back to your desk so that you can scroll through memes for the rest of the afternoon.

So never let meetings control your life, because they're certainly not worth it. Learn how to cut them short, and make sure to stick around just long enough so that no one suspects that you've literally been praying for a tornado to come and pulverize your office building. Always remember: either you end the meeting or the meeting ends you.

PART 6

Surviving the Day-to-Day

(Lord, Give Me the Strength)

They say that life is what happens to us when we're making other plans. But in the workplace, life is what happens to us between meetings and panic attacks. To say that day-to-day life in the workplace can be challenging is an understatement.

But a life committed to the workplace need not be a punishment, and there are ways to make it bearable, as long as you're willing to focus on what's most important in life: your own immediate needs and desires. Only the people who put their well-being first will survive with their psyche intact, while the strivers will burn out, give up, or become successful and fulfilled because they achieved their dreams through hard work and perseverance.

The following chapters will tackle this conundrum head-on and give you the tools needed to make the most of the aspects of the workplace that are often ignored in favor of shinier objects. When it comes down to it, it's the things that happen day to day that can *really* wear you down. But don't worry. If you look hard enough, there are ways to get around anything, so long as you're willing to be a bit shameless—which, as we both know, you definitely are.

Organizing Your Calendar
While Leaving Time to Cry

At work, much of our daily life is guided by a calendar—a chart that breaks down our months, weeks, and days into small blocks of emotional pain, helping to steer us from one unpleasant experience to the next, ensuring that we derive as little pleasure as possible, to the benefit of a corporate monolith that cares little for the human, political, and environmental toll left in its sociopathic wake.

While the calendar can dictate much of what we can get away with, it's not infallible, and with the right approach, it can be wrangled into submission. In fact, a tamed calendar can mean the difference between a tolerable week and one that requires maximum effort (bad!). So don't click "accept" on that calendar invite without trying to weasel your way out of it first—you might not succeed, but where there's a will (to avoid work), there's a way.

TIPS TO HELP YOU ORGANIZE
YOUR CALENDAR

They (don't ask who "they" are) say that an empty calendar is a good calendar, but in the workplace, an empty calendar leaves you wide open for assignments. That's why it's important to *look* busy, while tailoring your schedule to suit your personal comfort. Here are some calendar organization tips:

Tip #1: Make time for your morning routine

Too many people schedule meetings and other demanding tasks early in the day instead of making time for their routine. You should always prioritize a good start to your morning by setting aside time for a healthy breakfast, a half hour of meditation, or ten minutes of slapping your palm against your bedroom wall while screaming, "Why? Why? Why?" Ignore a good morning routine at your own peril.

Tip #2: Break your schedule into blocks

Instead of trying to do a hundred different things throughout the day, break the day into blocks of time devoted to specific activities. For instance, you might block off the hours between 10:00 a.m. and noon for responding to emails from your probation officer, and then 1:00 to 4:00 p.m. for trying to eavesdrop on your manager's calls. The key is to set aside time to focus on specific tasks instead of trying to multitask.

Tip #3: Say no to everything

Rather than taking the traditional approach and agreeing to everything thrown your way, you should do the exact opposite and turn down literally every single invitation that comes to your inbox unless the sender can convince (or force) you to do otherwise.

Budget meeting? Declined.

Brainstorming session? Declined.

Free company-wide lunch? Accepted, of course.

The key is to put the onus on the host, the same way our court system puts the onus on the prosecution to prove their case. If they can't get you to attend the meeting, then was it *really* that important to begin with?

Tip #4: Avoid setting appointments back to back

If you want your workday to be smooth sailing, then you should avoid setting multiple appointments back to back. Instead, space them out throughout the day or, preferably, the week, ensuring that you have at least a few hours of downtime every day. If you want to take it a step further, change the year on each appointment, spacing the meetings out throughout the decade. You probably won't get away with it, but if anyone asks why you never showed up, you can just point to the schedule and get yourself off the hook.

Tip #5: Keep your calendar to yourself

The reason why so many employees are inundated with calendar invites is because they give other people access to their calendar. Rather than share your schedule in an open and collaborative way, restrict access completely, ensuring that no one knows what you've got planned at any given moment. By doing this, not only will you take away people's ability to force you into meetings and appointments, but you'll allow yourself to claim that your schedule is jam packed, helping you to avoid assignments and live a life of leisure instead.

Tip #6: Color-code your calendar

A great way to stay organized is to color-code your calendar, assigning a unique color for a specific type of task. For instance, if an activity is important, like lunch, you can code it red. That way, anything else that's equally important can also be coded in red. Inversely, activities that aren't important can be coded in blue, so things like responding to emails, attending team meetings, and the core responsibilities of your job can be coded in blue. It's a simple process, but it helps.

Tip #7: Make time for tears

It's important to set aside time for self-care, and there's no better remedy for what ails the modern employee than a good crying session. You can schedule a half hour for crying in the early after-noon, or to be more efficient, you can schedule six or seven five-minute crying breaks throughout the day. To make the most of your daily breakdowns, label them as "crying" in the calendar. That way, nobody will ask questions or try to assign any extra work to you during those intervals.

DAILY SCHEDULE

7:00 AM – 7:45 AM	WAKE UP AND STARE AT CEILING IN DESPAIR
8:00 AM – 9:15 AM	GROW INCREASINGLY ANGRY WHILE SITTING IN TRAFFIC
9:30 AM – 10:00 AM	ARRIVE AT WORK THIRTY MINUTES LATE AND IMMEDIATELY EAT LUNCH
10:00 AM – 11:45 AM	SURF THE WEB WHILE CHECKING OVER SHOULDER FOR MANAGER
12:00 PM – 1:00 PM	EAT SECOND LUNCH FROM RESTAURANT YOU SWORE YOU'D NEVER GO TO AGAIN
1:00 PM – 2:30 PM	CARB COMA
2:30 PM – 2:40 PM	WORK
2:40 PM – 3:00 PM	CHECK SOCIAL MEDIA AND HAVE A SNACK AS REWARD FOR DOING WORK
3:00 PM – 4:00 PM	TENSION-FILLED MEETING WITH ABRASIVE AND UNCHARISMATIC COWORKERS
4:00 PM – 4:47 PM	DINNER BRAINSTORMING SESSION
4:47 PM	SNEAK OUT EARLY
5:00 PM – 6:00 PM	DINNER
6:00 PM – 11:00 PM	STARE INTO THE ABYSS
11:15 PM	BEDTIME

FINAL THOUGHTS

While it's the bane of some people's existence, a calendar need not be the source of your frustration or misery—a responsibility that should be left to your manager. Staying on top of your calendar and organizing it the way *you* want to can transform an otherwise miserable workweek into a more organized miserable workweek. Except for those few vacation days your company mercifully grants you every year, as long as you're at work, the best you can hope for is a somewhat bearable day.

The point, then, isn't to completely transform your role through your calendar but to mold it in accordance with your personal shortcomings and to take small victories as they come. You won't be able to get out of every responsibility, but you'll be able to get out of some, and that's always worth the effort. So the next time your calendar fills up with appointments you'd do anything to avoid, make up an excuse, hit the "decline" button, and log out of the system altogether. Mind over matter—if you don't mind, then it doesn't really matter.

Deadlines: Are They Important or Merely Suggestions?

Having to do things you don't want to do for money is bad enough but made much worse when there are arbitrary points in time by which a task must be completed. These narrow fields of time are called deadlines, and they make it much more difficult to drag out projects for maximum enjoyment, forcing us instead to buckle down and get things done under threat of reprimand or termination. It's not unlike a hostage situation, except our paychecks are the hostages, and work is the ransom payment.

But how seriously should we take deadlines, and is there anything that can be done to mitigate their impact on our prime web-surfing hours? The answer is complicated and will mostly depend on how gullible your manager is. But one thing is for sure: deadlines are never a good thing, and the more times you can break each deadline without getting fired, the happier you'll be.

If you're dead set on adhering to your manager's timetable, then you'll want to try not to miss any of the deadlines they've set. Here are some tips to help you become a better suck-up:

Tip #1: Break down goals into smaller daily tasks
When facing a deadline, a big assignment can seem incredibly daunting. That's why breaking it down into smaller, daily tasks can make it more manageable and allow you to complete it one piece

at a time. For instance: if you're required to write a one-thousand-word report, break it down into a daily goal of one word per day. That way, you will finish the report in a thousand days without so much as breaking a sweat.

Tip #2: Use a checklist

To better manage your goals, put together a checklist to organize your tasks and check them off after you complete each one. That way, the positive feeling you'll get from completing each task will give you more motivation to power through your remaining goals. Similarly, you can create a handful of fake tasks and pretend that you've completed them, checking off each one to make yourself feel like you've been extremely productive.

Tip #3: Move the deadline

Deadlines are a problem because they put a timetable on your efforts, forcing you to adhere to the ticking clock. The solution, therefore, is to move the deadline whenever it gets too close, buying yourself more time and never having to face the consequences of your actions. Deadlines can be moved a number of ways, whether through polite requests, manipulation, or begging. Just keep in mind that each time a deadline is moved, it becomes more difficult to do it again.

Tip #4: Ignore the deadline

Another option when faced with a daunting deadline is to ignore it, pretending that it doesn't exist and continuing to work at your own (extremely slow) pace. There are risks involved with this strategy, of course, but the sheer brazenness can sometimes pay off, essentially daring your coworkers to do something about your unwillingness to adhere to their rigid guidelines. They say rules were made to be broken, and a deadline sure as hell sounds like a rule, doesn't it?

Tip #5: Work when you feel most productive

People have different times throughout the day when they feel most productive. Some are able to get their best work done first thing in the morning, while others take longer to warm up and feel most productive in the afternoon or in the evening before bed. It can help to tailor your working schedule accordingly, attacking the hardest tasks whenever you have the most energy. And if you *never* feel productive, then it's probably best to never do any work, since it's obviously not meant to be.

Tip #6: Set aside uninterrupted time to work on your goals

With all the demands of work and your personal life, it can be difficult to find uninterrupted time to sit down and focus on your tasks. When faced with a deadline, you should carve out dedicated blocks to move your project forward, whether on a daily, weekly, or monthly basis. During these blocks, make sure to let others know you're not to be disturbed, whether it's your coworker, probation officer, or the long-lost child you fathered down in Florida in the late '90s. This time is dedicated to work, and all other distractions should be ignored.

Tip #7: Bribe a coworker to complete your assignment

When a deadline feels like it's too much to bear, you can always bribe a coworker to do the work for you, freeing you up to focus on more important things, like counting the recessed lights above your desk. You will, of course, have to part with some of your (not-so) hard-earned money, but it might be worth it not to be burdened by deadlines. After all, haven't you suffered enough?

FINAL THOUGHTS

While advocates might say that deadlines help keep people on track and ensure they remain productive, everybody else knows the truth: deadlines got their name because they make us wish we were dead. Having to do an assignment is bad enough, but when it's paired with a hard deadline, it's practically unbearable. That's why missing, avoiding, and ignoring deadlines has become so trendy—there are plenty of better things to do than worry about an arbitrary date due to your company's "desire to remain profitable."

So, if you're ever assigned a major project with a hard deadline, don't panic—it's not the end of the world. In fact, there's even a bright side to having a deadline: it can make you appreciate all those moments when you weren't being forced to work against the clock—gratitude is important! So the next time your manager tries to interrupt your life of leisure by giving you a deadline, don't get angry. She's just doing her job (which is to try to ruin your life). Instead, smile, say thank you, and then do anything and everything possible to meet the deadline, or to get yourself out of the assignment—the choice is yours.

The Commute to Work: Too Long but Never Really Long Enough

For those of us who aren't blessed with the ability to work from home, the most unpleasant part of every morning (besides opening your eyes and realizing the sweet release of death hasn't liberated you from this nightmare) is the trek to work known as the commute, which sounds a lot quainter than it actually is. A commute can be short or long, easy or difficult, violent or peaceful. The one thing a commute cannot be, however, is enjoyable—not for long anyway.

Most commutes are incredibly taxing, both physically and mentally, as evidenced by the gloomy faces of train, bus, and subway riders, all of whom look like they've just been told that the food they ordered was accidentally delivered to someone else (this really sucks by the way). But the one bright spot of commuting is the downtime before work, which allows people to clear their heads and get themselves mentally prepared for the office and the mind-numbing eight hours that await them once they step foot inside that carpeted chamber of gloom. This is, therefore, the paradox of commuting: it always feels too long, but it never really feels quite long enough.

• • •

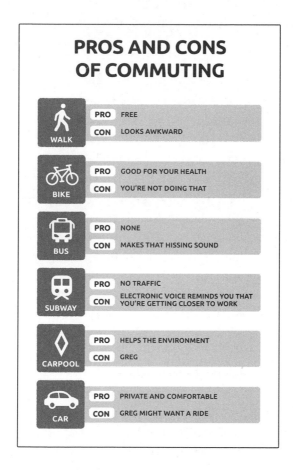

HOW TO MAKE YOUR COMMUTE BETTER

Thankfully, there are steps you can take in order to improve your daily commute. Here are a few:

Step #1: Make sure you're comfortable

If you're going to spend time in the car or on a bus or train, you should make sure your experience is a pleasant one. If driving, make sure to buy the most expensive car you can possibly afford, even if it will put you into crippling debt for the next decade. Your personal comfort is more important than you or your family's financial well-being, so make sure to act accordingly. If you're taking public transportation, sprawl out in your seat, taking up two or three spaces if you have to, so long as *you're* comfortable for the whole trip. By ensuring that you're able to relax, your commute will become less stressful, and you'll be able to recharge properly.

Step #2: Walk or bike to work when possible

Most of us don't get enough exercise, and the commute to work can offer a great opportunity to get your heart going. If you live within walking or cycling distance, skipping the car can be a healthy option, whether you choose to trek on foot or ride in on two wheels. Forgoing a vehicle or public transportation can also create more opportunities for financial gain, as getting clipped by a car while walking or cycling can lead to a significant payout from lawsuit settlements (assuming you survive). In either case, it's a bit of a win-win.

Step #3: Read or listen to podcasts

Spending a lot of time on the road won't be as bad if you incorporate entertainment into the experience, whether it's listening to an audiobook or podcast. Not only can you catch up on your reading, but you can also learn lots of new stuff, unless you choose this book, which really won't teach you anything useful (just being honest here!). In any case, many commuters use their travel time to catch up on reading and listening, and it can help you temporarily forget that you're on the way to (or on the way home from) a place that's slowly draining your lifeblood, one depressing drop at a time.

Step #4: Get a head start on your day

Since you're already headed to work, the morning commute can be a great time to tackle some assignments. Whether you respond to emails on your phone or pop open the laptop and dive into heavier work, you can get a lot more out of your commute by using the time to be productive. (We both know there is no way you're ever going to do this, but we had to include it in this section, so just go with it, please.) Getting ahead of the workday can help you stay on top of your tasks and might even allow you to leave early.

Step #5: Practice mindfulness

Studies have shown that people who practice mindfulness experience less stress and more life satisfaction than others. The morning commute can be the perfect time to practice mindfulness; but, unfortunately, no one really knows what mindfulness means, even if they pretend to. Apparently, it has something to do with meditation and trying to forget how miserable you are for a few minutes at a time, but it's all quite vague; so if you want to close your eyes and try to squeeze a few drops of serotonin from your brain on your way to work, then go right ahead.

Step #6: Switch things up

Doing the same commute day in and day out can become tedious, so it helps to switch things up every now and then. Instead of following the same route to work, take a detour, and drive through one of the nicer neighborhoods you could be living in if you weren't a chronic underachiever held back by your numerous shortcomings. Or, if you're used to taking the train, drive in every once in a while. This will offer a change of scenery and give you more privacy for your morning breakdown.

Step #7: Carpool with someone else

Carpooling with a coworker is not only cost efficient, it's also great for the environment. Many people choose to carpool because it saves money on gas and can make the commute to work more enjoyable—if you're the type of person who's actually interested in human interaction before 11:00 a.m. There's nothing quite like spending your morning hours listening to your coworker breathing heavily next to you as you inch closer to the bane of your existence, and if you can save a few bucks doing it, why not team up with someone else?!

FINAL THOUGHTS

Like shaving, commuting is a necessary evil. And just like shaving, we usually wait until the last possible minute to start our commute, hoping to absorb every drop of freedom available to us, the morning hours being no exception. Whether you live close to work or far away, a commute is what you make it; it can be an unpleasant ritual or an opportunity to plan the insider trading scheme that will finally make you rich—it's up to you.

And if you're the type of person who hates commuting, and there's no opportunity for you to find a remote job, don't fret, because it's all about mindset. A simple shift in your thinking can make your commute tolerable, even pleasant at times. All you have to do is remember that the unpleasant feelings you have when you're in the office all day long just start a bit earlier when you're forced to commute. And the sooner you accept your fate in its depressing entirety, the better off you'll (sort of) be.

The Gym and Other Office Perks You'll Never Use

As the workplace has evolved, employers have been forced to compete for talent, attempting to lure qualified prospects using all available methods, except paying people enough to have a good life. In addition to (or despite) salary and benefits, many companies offer perks, small extras meant to entice potential employees to join up and to forget that when they were a child they had hopes and dreams they believed they would one day achieve.

Perks, however, tend to appear much better on the surface than they really are, and if you look a bit closer, they usually don't stand up to scrutiny. That's not to say they don't have *any* value. But when it comes down to it, perks are much better in theory than in practice, sort of like hard work (you know it's true). And if you look at perks in context, they're usually inexpensive but shiny objects that can distract from more important things, like salary. Nevertheless, perks can come in handy, and it's important to understand exactly which ones you have available to you.

THE DIFFERENT TYPES OF PERKS

Perks can range in their impact and value. Here are some of the more common perks offered by employers and how they work.

- **Casual dress code.** This perk allows you to skip the business attire and wear whatever you want to the office, as if putting on a pair of jeans will make you forget that your supervisor is literally insane.
- **Free snacks.** Many companies provide free snacks to their employees, spending upwards of tens of dollars on obscure, bottom-of-the-barrel treats that have since been discontinued by their manufacturers for you to enjoy.
- **Gym membership or reimbursement.** Companies first create an environment where you're almost certain to get out of shape, then provide a free gym membership to help you burn off all the weight they've helped you to gain. It's a vicious circle.
- **Pet insurance.** While most companies won't offer health insurance good enough to ensure that you won't go bankrupt if you become seriously ill, they *will* offer this same type of insurance for your pet. At least your labradoodle won't have to sell his laptop to afford the out-of-pocket premium.
- **Ping-Pong table.** Putting a Ping-Pong table or other tabletop games in the office can show potential hires that the company is hip, fun, and thinks you're dumb enough to accept a 40 percent pay cut in exchange for two wooden paddles and a tiny plastic ball.
- **Standing desks.** These desks are actually a fairly decent perk since they can take some of the strain off your lower back. Unfortunately, they don't do anything for the emotional strain of knowing that you peaked in high school.
- **Company fun runs (5K/10K).** In no way, shape, or form is this an actual perk.
- **Mentor program.** If you've always wanted a mentor, then this perk is perfect for you. If you're not a complete weirdo, however, then this is just another opportunity for the company to try to brainwash you into subservience.
- **Tuition reimbursement.** It's tough to criticize this perk, but we're willing to give it a shot. The problem isn't that you'll get

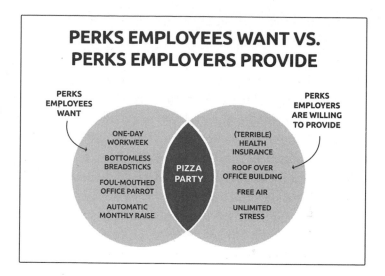

money to put toward your education. The problem is that you're usually required to remain at the company, or you'll be forced to repay the reimbursement. What's the point of going back to school if you can't immediately quit your job when you're done?!

PERKS ALL COMPANIES SHOULD OFFER

If companies were serious about retaining employees, they would eschew the more trivial perks and offer the following ones instead:

- **Free back rubs from your office crush.** Everyone knows that Eric from legal is married, but if he was allowed (mandated?) to give you a deep-tissue massage at least once a week, there's no way you'd even consider looking for a job somewhere else.
- **A one-hour workweek.** Imagine how focused and productive you would be if the obsolete five-day workweek was replaced by the more manageable one-hour workweek. Productivity and quality of work would skyrocket.
- **CEO-for-a-Day Day.** If a company wanted to retain top talent, they would offer this perk, which would allow every person from

the company to serve as the chief executive officer for exactly one day. Not only would this improve morale, it would also provide valuable on-the-job training to those with higher aspirations.

- **Assigned bathroom stalls.** One of the worst things about the office is being forced to share a bathroom with God-knows-who. Assigned bathroom stalls would give everyone their own private sanctuary, where they could go to weep, handle bodily functions, and hide from their boss in peace.
- **Complimentary Botox/plastic surgery.** Workplace stress can take its toll on our bodies, causing wrinkles, weight gain, and accelerated aging. That's why free plastic surgery would be such a valuable perk. If we knew that our stress-related skin needs would be covered, we'd be less apt to try to get out of highly demanding assignments.

FINAL THOUGHTS

As we mentioned earlier, life is all about deceit, and workplace perks are merely small deceptions designed to convince you that you're getting something valuable for free. The harsh truth, however, is that these seemingly valuable perks cost a mere fraction of what your employer can extract from your labor (well, maybe not *your* labor, but the labor of someone who actually does what they're supposed to do).

But don't let that deter you from hoovering up every single benefit you can get your grubby hands on, because you never want to say no to "free" stuff. Just make sure to remember that some Ivy League dweeb who sleeps with his Brooks Brothers socks on has done the math and decided that the perks they're offering will cost a mere pittance when compared to what (they think) you'll bring to the table. So take what you can get, then try to take a little more, but remember: they'll always expect something in return.

Vacation Time:
Strategic Use for Maximum Joy

I f they could, companies would keep you chained to your desk for twenty-four hours a day, 365 days a year, injecting you with various stimulants to ensure you stay awake long enough to complete their meaningless tasks before they toss the empty husk that once contained your soul out through the garbage chute and replace you with a fresher specimen.

Thankfully, there are laws against this sort of thing. Not only that, but many employers will actually give you time off to take a

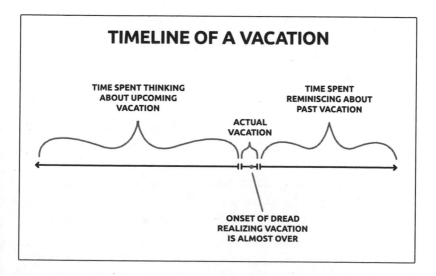

TIMELINE OF A VACATION

TIME SPENT THINKING
ABOUT UPCOMING
VACATION

TIME SPENT
REMINISCING ABOUT
PAST VACATION

ACTUAL
VACATION

ONSET OF DREAD
REALIZING VACATION
IS ALMOST OVER

vacation, giving you a week or two to taste the sweet freedom you'd experience if you'd been born into a successful family. But don't let this apparent act of generosity fool you. Vacation time isn't given out of the kindness of your employer's heart; it's given because, if it were not, there would be a dangerous employee uprising with pitchforks, bubble wrap, and other weird stuff. So take your vacation time. Use every last day. But remember that when it runs out, you have to go back. Tragic.

To extract every possible bit of joy from your allotted vacation time, you need to be strategic about it. Here are some tips to ensure you don't leave a single second of happiness on the table:

Tip #1: Use weekends to boost your vacation time

If you plan correctly, weekends can actually help extend your vacation time. Rather than starting a vacation mid-week, start it on Monday and end it on Friday, so that you can take advantage of the consecutive days off. Or maybe you need to start it on Friday, and end it on Monday? It's actually really confusing to try to figure it out, but there's probably a way to make it work.

Tip #2: Plan vacations around holidays

Another way to get the most out of vacation days is to schedule them around holidays, so that you can prolong your time away from work. The downside to doing this is that most other people have the same idea, so you're likely to find yourself at the beach or an amusement park with thousands of others, reminding you that you're just a small cog in the wheel, an ant slowly marching toward oblivion.

Tip #3: Spread your vacation hours throughout the year

Try to spread your vacations throughout the year instead of using them all in one pop. This will ensure that you don't run out of vacation days, and that you don't go too long without taking a break. Because if there's one thing for certain, it's that you're pathologically unable to do more than a few consecutive weeks of work before you completely fall apart.

Tip #4: Try to take time off during your company's busy season

If you're going to use your vacation time, it makes sense to use it when your company needs you most. That way, you'll be out of the office when the workload is the heaviest, leaving your coworkers to pick up your slack. To do this, you'll need to plan ahead and book your vacation time early, but if you have enough foresight, you'll be relaxing on a lawn chair while the people you work with are cursing your name.

Tip #5: Use it or lose it

Some companies allow you to roll your vacation time into the next year, while others don't, forcing you to forfeit any accrued hours if you don't use them. This is why it's so important to understand your company's vacation policy and to use your hours accordingly. You're already giving up your time, physical health, the best years of your life, your morals, your conscience, and most of your soul, so why give up the hours you're due?

Tip #6: Take one giant vacation

Another option for making the most of your vacation time is to use it all up in one long megavacation. The downside, of course, is that you won't have any time off left for the rest of the year. But think of how much fun you'll have spending two consecutive weeks away from the office. That's two weeks to unwind, two weeks to relax, two weeks to meet a wealthy stranger and assume their identity after pushing them off a boat during an impromptu fishing trip—a lot can happen in fourteen days.

Tip #7: Make sure to unplug

Vacations are meaningless if we can't unplug from the daily distractions of our busy lives. Whenever you take time off, make sure to unplug and give yourself space to clear your mind. Close your laptop and stop all push notifications. Better yet, turn off your cell phone completely, and don't tell your coworkers where you'll be staying. Before leaving the house, unplug your fridge and all of your lamps, and the microwave too. Disconnect your car's battery, and remove the one that's in your watch. If you're going to take time off, make sure it's on your terms.

FINAL THOUGHTS

Vacations can be wonderful, but they usually come at a price. That price is the nauseous feeling you get when you remember that you'll have to go back to the office, an unpleasant feeling that reminds you that you aren't truly free, and that a petty tyrant named Julie decides what you can and can't do with your time, as if you're a child and not a full-grown childlike adult.

Nevertheless, having vacation time is better than the alternative, and there's no reason not to make the most of it. You deserve a break after many long months of doing the absolute bare minimum. So go ahead and book that trip you've been dreaming about. If your employer can remain successful while you're there, then they'll definitely be fine when you're not.

Annual Reviews, Salary Negotiations/Existential Dread

Throughout the term of your employment, you should expect to go through a review process, usually held annually, during which time your manager will determine whether your work has met expectations and whether you deserve a promotion and/or a salary increase. While we both know you deserve neither, it's in your best interests to play an active role in this process and advocate on your own behalf. As they say, the squeaky wheel gets the grease, and you are very squeaky indeed.

The best way to tackle this process is head-on: be open, honest, and direct, without going into too much detail about what you've been working on and how much effort you've been putting in. Speak in generalities and use the buzzwords we went over in chapter 4. The goal is to steer your employer toward an optimistic picture of your productivity and away from the volume and quality of the work you've actually done.

HOW TO NAIL A PERFORMANCE REVIEW

Instead of trying to wing it, you should take the time to properly prepare for your performance review. After all, it will affect how much money you make, which is literally the most important thing in life. Here are some tips to help you nail your next performance review:

Tip #1: Lie

The number one thing you can do to improve your performance review is to lie, and to lie convincingly enough that your manager will think you're being sincere. Lie about how hard you've been working, lie about how committed you are to the organization, and lie about the adversity you've had to overcome in your personal life. Lie until you believe your own lies; but do not, under any circumstances, admit that you're lying.

Tip #2: Ask for feedback

During a performance review, it's important to look like you're trying to improve. You can do this by asking for feedback about your performance and about what you can do to become a better employee. The feedback itself isn't really important, since you have no intention of doing anything differently after the review, but by asking the right questions, you can make it appear as if you're committed to personal development and long-term success.

Tip #3: Don't get defensive

Since you're a terrible (absolutely dreadful) employee, you'll likely get some negative feedback during your review. Make sure you don't take it personally, since every employee will get constructive criticism, not just the ones who spend the majority of their working hours looking at memes. Instead of getting defensive, try listening, and asking questions in order to get more context about how terrible you really are. Getting defensive will only hurt your case.

Tip #4: Ask for support

Another great way to position yourself as someone who is looking to improve is to ask for help. This will not only show that you're taking initiative but will also make your supervisor feel valued. Showing vulnerability is a great way to gain sympathy, which can then be used to manipulate people into letting you do what you want. So don't be afraid to ask for help—it's a surefire way to buy yourself more time to relax.

Tip #5: Thank your supervisor

Be sure to thank your supervisor throughout the review, even if it might feel a bit awkward. By thanking them over and over again, you will make it more difficult for them to be too aggressive in their criticism and will temper any anger they might have at your shockingly poor performance. Thank them for inviting you to the review and thank them for every single question they ask. Thank them for the water, for the feedback, and the opportunity. Thank them for believing in you. Thank them for being who they are. How can anybody be angry at somebody who is so polite?

Tip #6: Make empty promises

While most performance reviews focus on the past, ultimately, they're more concerned with the future. This is why it's critically important to over-promise during your performance review, and to convince your supervisors that you're going to do things that you have no intention of ever doing. Pick an initiative that has been causing your manager a lot of grief and tell them that you'll see it through. Volunteer for more work. Explain that you're more motivated than ever. Then, after the performance review is over, go back to your desk and start looking for another job.

Tip #7: Don't forget to smile

Nobody likes a Debbie Downer. In fact, irrationally happy people tend to thrive in the workplace, spreading their disgusting joy around the office like pollen and masking their intractable stupidity with a delectable wide-mouthed grin. While there's nothing short of an entire pharmacy that could turn you into one of these people, you should at least do your best to pretend during your performance review. Smile when your supervisor is talking. Smile when it's your turn to speak. Smile when they confront you for using the company credit card to buy specious cryptocurrency. And smile when the police put you in handcuffs and take you away to jail.

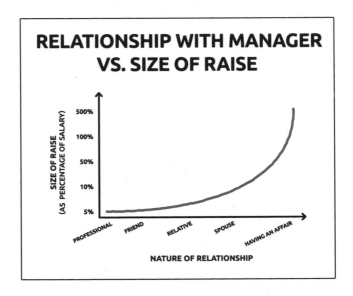

HOW TO ASK FOR A RAISE

Annual reviews can be the perfect time to ask for a raise. Here are some tips:

- Research how much somebody in your role is expected to earn.
- Try to approach your manager when they're in a good mood.
- When possible, use (forged) documents to strengthen your case.
- Wear your worst outfit so that it looks like you can't afford decent clothes.

- Be clear, concise, and vaguely threatening.
- Have a backup plan in case things don't go as planned. Crying is not a backup plan.
- Be prepared to offer an ultimatum. But also be prepared for your supervisor to gladly accept your ultimatum and show you the door.

FINAL THOUGHTS

As unpleasant as they might be, annual reviews are your best opportunity to get a raise. Management understands that they have to throw their employees a few scraps each year or they'll start to lose valuable employees (not you) and will become the laughingstock of their Botox-faced peers at the local country club, a place you'll never ever be invited to, ever. But what's good for the goose is good for the gander, so the next time you're asked to do your annual review, make sure to go for broke—you have nothing to lose by trying.

So take the annual review seriously, even if the thought of reliving the last year of your life fills you with a profound sense of sadness. You can't change the past, but you can change the future, for a few hours, until you fall into your natural state of laziness again. But if you manage to nail your review, at least you'll be able to increase your income a bit. It won't take the pain away completely, but it will allow you to mask it by buying things, which is almost as good, right?

Work-Life Balance and Its Direct Correlation with Being Broke

As children, we learn about wondrous fairy tales such as Cinderella and Rumpelstiltskin, made-up stories designed to enchant and delight us, and to show us that there might be more to the world than meets the eye. The most pervasive fairy tale, however, is the idea of work-life balance—because unless you're working from home, on a part-time basis, while getting paid a full salary, there's really no such thing.

To be sure, some people *do* manage to strike a balance, but usually it's because they don't have much of a life to begin with. It's not that difficult to spend forty or fifty hours at work when the only thing you have to come home to is a big-screen TV and a dozen unanswered Tinder messages. But for everybody else, work-life balance is the Holy Grail. Let's delve into it.

HOW TO ACHIEVE BETTER WORK-LIFE BALANCE

Short of going to prison, there are few ways to feed and house yourself without having to work. Keeping this in mind, the best any of us can hope for is to attain a *certain* level of balance between our personal and professional lives. Here are some tips to get things on a more even keel:

1. Do less work

One surefire way to have better work-life balance is to do less actual work. By reducing the amount of work you do down to the absolute bare minimum, you'll be happier, healthier, and more fulfilled. While your supervisor might find this approach to be less than ideal, it's still the gold standard for work-life balance and will ensure that stressful, unpleasant work doesn't get in the way of your life of leisure.

2. Take frequent breaks

It's important to take breaks throughout the day, especially when you're looking to improve your work-life balance. Make it a point to take at least two fifteen-minute breaks away from relaxing in order to do some of the work your employer requires. By taking at least a half hour away from relaxing next to the pool, you'll maintain a great work-life balance and have some productivity to point to if your coworkers ever try to accuse you of never getting anything done.

3. Play to your strengths

Instead of trying to be everything to everybody, try to be nothing to nobody by playing to your (few) strengths. Rather than accepting every assignment that comes your way, focus on the ones that play to your strengths, such as frequency of mood swings per day and number of calories consumed at lunch. Don't waste time on things you're not good at—that list is *way* too long.

4. Make time for exercise

A healthy body means a fresh mind, which is why high achievers make time for daily exercise, strengthening their bodies and using their energy to become better than the rest of us. You should also make time for exercise, but not to work out, which is actually super hard and definitely unpleasant. Instead, use "exercise time" as an excuse to come in late and leave early. Most workplaces are now prioritizing a healthy lifestyle, and "going to the gym" is a perfect excuse to get out of doing things you don't want to do.

5. Focus on your social life

You should always have something to look forward to, and spending time with friends is not one of those things. It's exhausting to hear about people's promotions, engagements, and home purchases, especially since, deep down, you know you're better than them. Instead, try to make friends with people who know nothing about you, so you can hide the fact that you're a chronic underachiever behind a complex wall of lies. This way, you'll be left feeling refreshed, rather than jealous and inadequate.

6. Always come in late and leave early

While a few minutes here and there might not seem like much, over time, they tend to add up. This is why it's so important to come in to work a few minutes late, and to leave a few minutes before the end of your scheduled shift, *every single day*. This same logic should apply when going to (or coming back from) lunch, and on any and every break the company provides. By stealing ten or twenty minutes per day, you can give yourself an extra few days off per year!

JOBS THAT OFFER A GREAT WORK-LIFE BALANCE

While your job might not provide much in the way of work-life balance, there are many careers out there that do. Here are a few:

- unemployed
- heir to chocolate fortune
- bestselling writer (not us)
- unindicted financial fraud coconspirator
- ten-year sleep study participant

- pickpocket
- incredibly good-looking person who gets by on their looks
- guy who abandoned his family to start over in another state

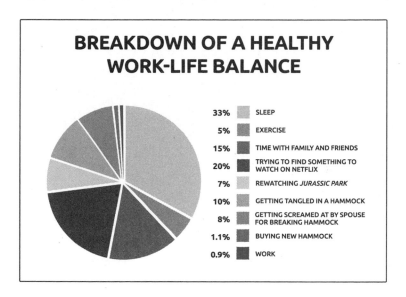

BREAKDOWN OF A HEALTHY WORK-LIFE BALANCE

33%	SLEEP
5%	EXERCISE
15%	TIME WITH FAMILY AND FRIENDS
20%	TRYING TO FIND SOMETHING TO WATCH ON NETFLIX
7%	REWATCHING *JURASSIC PARK*
10%	GETTING TANGLED IN A HAMMOCK
8%	GETTING SCREAMED AT BY SPOUSE FOR BREAKING HAMMOCK
1.1%	BUYING NEW HAMMOCK
0.9%	WORK

FINAL THOUGHTS

While we all wish we could find fulfilling jobs that offer the perfect mix of work and play, the best we can really hope for is a company disorganized enough to allow us to slip through the cracks and a manager aloof enough to let us get away with it. Work-life balance, therefore, isn't about perfection; it's about constantly gaming the system in your favor, in ways both big and small, obvious and subtle. Take what you can get and run with it, and never, ever quit.

And if you ever find yourself with less work-life balance than you'd hoped for, don't get upset—you're not alone. There are millions of people who feel like they're being worked to death while the overlords who control their fate sip champagne on massive yachts in the South of France. That's just the way it is, and the only thing you can do about it is to take the small wins as they come, whether it's grabbing the roast beef instead of the tuna when the company caters Panera for lunch or using Photoshop to create a fake advanced degree in order to land a higher-paying role. Do what you can and try not to worry about the rest.

PART 7

Termination of Employment

(Let's Pretend We Liked Each Other)

Like the temporary happiness of your childhood, sooner or later, everything must come to an end. The workplace is no exception, and the days of spending decades with a company before retiring with a pension and a gold watch are long over. These days, people switch jobs like you switch personalities, and there's nothing unusual about spending a year or two with a firm before moving on to greener pastures.

Leaving a job, however, tends to be a fraught and awkward process. In most cases, somebody walks away feeling betrayed, whether it's your employer who wouldn't blink twice if the roles were reversed or you, who has a persecution complex. It's rare for a termination of employment to go smoothly, but it's not unheard of, which is why it's important to remain professional even if you're desperate to play out the dramatic shouting scene you've pictured in your head a thousand times.

In the next chapters, we'll cover all aspects of moving on, from knowing when it's time to go, to looking for something new, to the right way to write a letter of resignation. Leaving a job doesn't have to be an unpleasant experience, but it probably will be since you and your employer are both immature and can't put aside your egos and petty jealousies long enough to act like professional adults. But what else can we say? Just do your best—someday it might be good enough.

Is It Time to Move On,
or Is It Just Indigestion?

At some point in your employment, you might get an uneasy feeling. It's a feeling that tells you something isn't quite right. This feeling will be different from the sense of distaste you felt after your first week on the job. It will be more poignant, like a damp blanket draped over your shoulders on a frigid September afternoon. Before you dismiss it as your run-of-the-mill anxiety, or the by-product of stuffing yourself full of beef every afternoon, you should ask yourself whether your time with your employer is drawing to a close.

When you get this feeling, you might be tempted to ignore it. After all, ignoring problems is the best way to make them go away. But unless you're one of the lucky few, this feeling will continue to grow, until it consumes you, rendering you unable to function at work, which is why you need to identify and examine it. Because when it's time to move on, your body will know it before your mind does.

SIGNS THAT IT'S TIME TO MOVE ON

While knowing when it's time to leave an employer isn't an exact science, there *are* some signs that might point to yes. Here are a few that you don't want to miss:

Sign #1: Every morning, you sit in your car with your face in your hands

One sure sign that it's time to move on is when you spend ten minutes every morning parked outside the office with your face in your hands. Though there might be other reasons for sobbing in your car every single morning, you can't overlook the fact that your job might be a contributing factor. If you find yourself screaming into your clenched fist every morning, it might just be time to look for another gig.

Sign #2: Someone offers you a better opportunity (because they don't really know you)

If a recruiter or another employer offers you a job with better pay or more opportunity for advancement because they don't know you're a terrible employee, then it might be time to move on. Staying stagnant in your career is a one-way ticket to mediocrity, and you only get so many chances to fool prospective employers about your talent and work ethic. So, if a better opportunity comes along, take it before they have a chance to learn the truth.

Sign #3: Your manager keeps emailing you with the subject line "Please leave"

This one can be a bit ambiguous, and you should be careful not to read too much into it, but when your supervisor sends a daily email with the subject line "You need to leave," or "We don't want you here anymore," then it might be time to start packing. Again, there's no guarantee that your tenure is coming to a close, but having somebody message you "GET OUT" in all caps every morning might be a sign that it's time to start looking for something new.

Sign #4: You're not being praised for every single thing you do

If you're not receiving effusive praise for every single task you manage to complete, no matter how small, then it might be time to look for the exit. Everybody wants to feel valued, and when your manager doesn't congratulate you for taking thirty seconds to respond to an email, it can feel like you're not an important member of the team. Once this starts happening, it's time to find a company that will congratulate you for every bit of menial effort you manage to squeeze out. Otherwise, it's unlikely that you'll ever truly feel appreciated.

Sign #5: You no longer need to be employed as a condition of your parole
You've put in the work, met regularly with your parole officer, and completed the hundreds of hours of court-mandated community

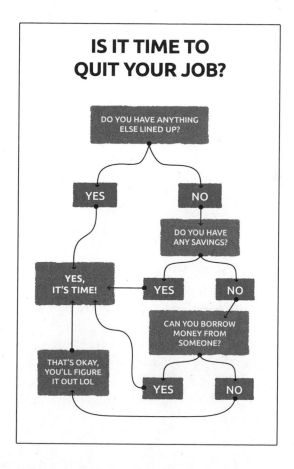

service, and now you're finally off the hook! Now is the perfect time to look for something new, since you can't get sent back to prison for quitting your job anymore. If ever there was a sign that it's time to switch employers, coming to the end of your parole is it, so dust off that résumé, come up with a good explanation for the failed background check, and you'll be starting a new role in no time.

Sign #6: You get a vague message in a fortune cookie that can be loosely interpreted as a sign

There is no better indicator that your time with an employer is coming to a close than a fortune cookie that vaguely alludes to something to do with moving on. Even if the fortune says nothing about a job or money, as long as it can be twisted into something resembling a link, you can be certain that it's time to start looking for another job. Never ignore the meaning behind a generic, mass-produced message.

FINAL THOUGHTS

Knowing when to quit can be difficult, but quitting itself is super easy and feels great. So don't be afraid to throw in the towel when work no longer brings you the joy that you feel you deserve, because there's nothing worse than being stuck in a job that's no longer a good fit. Remember: *you* are in charge of your destiny, along with a host of seemingly random circumstances over which you literally have no control at all.

Pay attention to the signs, no matter how subtle. If you experience even the slightest bit of discomfort, it might be time to get a fresh start somewhere new, because overcoming adversity takes a *ton* of effort—you've been warned. But before you march into your manager's office and give them a piece of your mind, make sure you've got something else lined up. In this next section, we'll show you how.

Looking for a New Job While Still Employed as If You're Some Sort of International Spy

J obs are like relationships: most people won't let go of one until they have another one lined up (I hate you, Kristen). That's why knowing how to look for another role while you're still employed is so important. If you're able to secure a position before moving on, you don't have to risk the $738 you've managed to put in your savings account over the last five years.

But job-hunting while working for somebody else can be tricky. There are lots of ways to get tripped up, and if your employer finds out you've been looking for an exit strategy, they won't be happy. That's why the key to looking for another job while you're still employed is the same as the key to every other type of success: lying.

TIPS FOR LOOKING FOR A NEW JOB WHILE YOU'RE STILL EMPLOYED

Before you start sending your résumé to every employer within a fifty-mile radius, you should take a step back and make sure you're doing things the right way. Here are some tips to help you look for a job while you already have one:

Tip #1: Keep it to yourself

While you might think you can trust your coworkers to keep a secret, it's best to play it safe and avoid telling anyone that you're looking for another job. Not only do you run the risk of it getting back to your supervisor, but you don't want to give your coworkers any ideas. The *only* person on the planet who should have a chance to be happy is you.

Tip #2: Never use company equipment

Though it can be tempting (and convenient) to use your company-issued computer to look for a new job, you will want to limit job searching to your personal devices. Company equipment should only be used for work and for anonymously filling out one-star reviews on your ex's small business page, *not* to look for a new role.

Tip #3: Find another reference

Since you don't want your current employer to know that you're seeking other opportunities, you'll want to find another reference willing to lie and say that you're a good employee. Check with past managers and see if they're willing to completely misrepresent your abilities, and let them know they might be hearing from a potential employer. Chances are, they'll agree to do it just to get you off the phone.

Tip #4: Try to schedule interviews during off hours

To avoid suspicion, try to schedule interviews with prospective employers before work, after work, or during your lunch break. In some cases, this might be impossible, which means you'll have to make up a believable excuse to get a few hours off. Some common excuses are a doctor's appointment, a family emergency, or accidentally being locked in the engine room of a departing cruise ship. As long as you make it believable, you should be fine.

Tip #5: Act normal at work

Even if you have one leg out the door, you should still proceed as if nothing has changed. This means you should continue to show up every day in a sullen mood, procrastinate for hours before grudgingly doing twenty minutes of actual work, and complain all day long about anything and everything, portraying yourself as a helpless victim and the only competent person in a company full of morons. As long as you keep doing what you've been doing, no one will be the wiser.

Tip #6: Ask your prospective employers to be discreet

It helps to involve your prospective employers in your lies, so don't be shy about asking them to be discreet. Most hiring managers understand that you'll want to keep your job search a secret, and you're unlikely to get much pushback. And since they're already keeping one secret for you, you can use the opportunity to confess the rest of your sins, unburdening yourself of the guilt you've been carrying since that warm summer night eighteen years ago. Free yourself by coming clean; it'll be worth it.

Tip #7: Be careful what you do online

While your current online search history is probably enough to cost you your job and any and all current and future relationships, you need to be extra careful when looking for a job. One wrong click of the mouse, and your coworkers and management could see your online activity, making it clear that you're looking to leave. Be mindful when browsing online. Even though it won't be anywhere near as embarrassing as the rest of your digital activity, it could still cost you your job.

FINAL THOUGHTS

Don't be afraid to look for a new job, even if you were lucky to get the one you have now. A successful career requires looking for opportunities and having a very rich father. On the other hand, staying in the same role for too long can lead to stagnation, and there's no way you're going to impress Liz Watkins at the upcoming high school reunion with your current job title.

Success requires climbing the corporate ladder, and oftentimes, that means switching employers. So don't shy away from switching jobs every few years, every year, every month, maybe even every week. Just be sure to do things the right way. A person who is currently employed is much more attractive to a prospective employer than one who is not. It's a sick and twisted rule, but the workplace is a sick and twisted place. So update your humiliating LinkedIn profile, send out that underwhelming résumé, and watch the calls and emails roll in. Hopefully, at least one of them isn't an instant rejection.

Getting Furloughed, Laid Off, Fired, Demoted, or Summarily Executed

In some cases, the decision of whether to leave will be made for you. There are many ways a company can get rid of you, whether through temporary processes like furloughs or permanent means like layoffs and terminations. In fact, some companies will intentionally try to make your time at work more unpleasant in an effort to get you to quit, though little do they know that you couldn't possibly be any more miserable than you already are now. In any case, if an employer wants you gone, there's little you can do about it except threaten to sue them using doctored emails and made-up statements.

This is why it's so important to understand your rights, or at least understand how to say "I know my rights" with enough conviction to make it sound believable. The truth, however, is that unless your employer clearly broke the law, you're unlikely to have any recourse. So perhaps the best thing to do might be to accept your fate and to spend a few months feeling sorry for yourself until you start getting collection notices. Because what doesn't kill you makes you stronger—until something eventually *does* kill you, so there's always that to look forward to.

• • •

THE DIFFERENCE BETWEEN THE EMPLOYMENT ACTIONS

It can be helpful to understand the different actions an employer can take to finally be rid of you. While their options are constrained by state and federal law, don't be fooled: if they want you out, they're not going to block you on every social media platform like your ex-girlfriend; they'll just take one of the following actions and never think about you again.

Furlough

A furlough is a mandatory temporary leave of absence after which you'll be expected to return to work. Employers usually rely on furloughs when they can't make payroll or when business is slow or when they want to play games with people's lives. The upside of a furlough is that you'll get some time off to pursue your weird and socially inappropriate hobbies. The downside is that you won't be paid for your time off.

Layoff

A layoff is a separation from employment due to a lack of available work. It can be temporary or permanent and is a type of termination that implies the employee is not to blame. The upside of a layoff is that it allows you to file for unemployment benefits and absolves you of any responsibility for your loss of work. The downside is, well—actually, there isn't much of a downside. You get to take some time off while collecting unemployment benefits. It's actually pretty sweet.

Firing

A firing is a separation from employment due to something that the company deems to be your fault. In your case, there are probably a thousand different things an employer could point to, so don't be too surprised. If you've been fired, make sure to get the reason for the termination in writing. That way, you can hang it up in your living room and stare at it whenever you need motivation to go through with your elaborate revenge scheme.

Managing Out

While not necessarily a direct action, an employer who wants to rid themselves of a problematic employee without going through the firing process might try an approach called "managing out." This refers to making an employee's life so unpleasant that they leave on their own accord. If you sense that this might be happening to you, you have only one option: fight back. Try to make your manager's life as miserable as possible but in a way that's perfectly legitimate. Ask questions about everything, constantly, hundreds of questions throughout the day. Pretend you don't understand even the most basic concepts, but frame your questions in such a way that they appear as if they're being asked out of a sense of obligation to get things right. While your time with the company is likely coming to a close regardless, you should at least make your manager's life as unpleasant as possible on your way out.

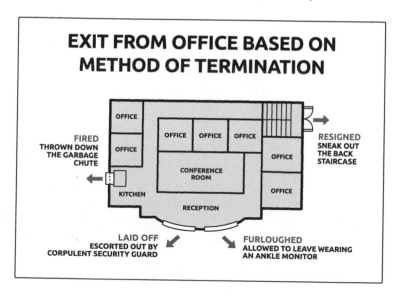

SIGNS THAT YOU MIGHT SOON BE TERMINATED

Sometimes, you can see your termination coming before it happens. The following signs may indicate that your employment will soon be coming to an end:

- You receive more than one negative performance review.
- Your boss no longer asks for your help.
- The company puts your personal belongings in a cardboard box every morning.
- Your coworkers start referring to you in the past tense.
- You have to enter the building through the back entrance in order to avoid security.
- Your boss wants to meet one-on-one frequently, and it's not because they're trying to hit on you.
- Someone with your same skill set and the same first and last name as you has just been hired.

FINAL THOUGHTS

The idea of losing a job that you rely on to pay your crushing monthly expenses can be scary. The fear of not knowing where your next paycheck is coming from tends to cause immense anxiety, though it means literally nothing to your employer, who will forget about you forever the second you step foot out the door.

This is why it's important to look out for yourself and to understand your options when it comes to the end of your employment. You have a choice: you can either view it as a negative and feel sorry for yourself, or you can use it as motivation to find a better job that you'll get fired from eventually as well. But no matter which option you choose, you should always remember that jobs come and go—but your negative attitude will always remain.

Writing a Letter of Resignation When You've Already Been Resigned from Day One

For some strange reason, it's important to remain professional even when severing ties with an employer. The way you leave a job matters, and it can mean the difference between a good reference and an honest one. A professional will bring their tenure to a close on a polite and respectful note, while someone who is not will create drama and try to cause as much damage as they can on their way out the door.

To be sure, it's possible to insult your manager and coworkers while remaining outwardly professional, as long as it's done subtly. After all, most people at work have perfected the art of the passive-aggressive swipe, so why shouldn't you be allowed to have some fun in your last few weeks on the job? Just be sure to mask your seething contempt with a thin veneer of professionalism. Otherwise, have at it!

THE IMPORTANCE OF GIVING NOTICE

Although not required by law, most employers expect you to give a two-week notice when you resign. A notice gives them time to transition your work over to someone else, find a replacement, and treat you like absolute garbage for the crime of thinking you can go work somewhere else. Regardless of whether you agree with it or not, you should always try to give notice, if only for the satisfaction of getting paid to do absolutely nothing for two weeks. Here are some tips for giving a two-week notice:

Tip #1: Pick the right time

You'll want to be mindful of circumstances when giving your notice, paying close attention to what's going on in the workplace. If you're in the middle of any major projects, or if the company is short-staffed and relying on you to carry the weight, then it's the absolute perfect time to put in your notice. Don't wait until the timing is off—put in your notice and move on.

Tip #2: Give your notice in person

Even though avoiding your manager is one of your most well-developed skills, you'll want to put it aside when giving your notice. A notice should be handed to your supervisor in person, rather than via email, and you should be able to witness their face turning red and their hands clenching into fists firsthand—this is the professional way to do it.

Tip #3: Keep it simple

You don't need to go overboard when composing a two-week notice. Keep it simple and stick to the facts, and avoid airing any grievances about the role or about management. The intent of the notice is simply to let your employer know that you'll be moving on. All other complaints and judgments should be reserved for a company-wide email sent out on the last day of your employment.

SAMPLE TWO-WEEK NOTICE

The following is an example of a professionally written two-week notice:

Dear Mr./Ms. Last Name,

I am writing to announce my resignation from [Company Name], effective two beautiful weeks from this date.

This was not an easy decision to make, but tbh, it wasn't a difficult one either lol. The past ten years have been very rewarding, just not for me. I've enjoyed working with you and the rest of the team and will miss using the company credit card to order Uber Eats.

Thank you for the opportunity. I wish you and the company all the best (sarcasm). If I can be of any help during the transition, please make sure it's a last resort.

Sincerely,

Your Signature

Your Typed Name

TIMELINE OF TWO-WEEK NOTICE

NO WORK GETS DONE WHATSOEVER

DAY 1 — NOTICE GIVEN TO MANAGER

DAY 2 — WORD MAKES ITS WAY AROUND THE OFFICE

DAY 4 — MANAGER STARTS GIVING YOU DIRTY LOOKS

DAY 7 — DESPERATE COWORKER ASKS IF THEY CAN COME WITH YOU

DAY 13 — NO ONE WILL EVEN LOOK IN YOUR DIRECTION

KEY CARD DEACTIVATED

DAY 14 — COWORKERS PRETEND THAT THEY'LL MISS YOU

QUITTING WITHOUT NOTICE

In some cases, you might want to resign without giving notice. While this might be frowned upon by people who love to frown, there's nothing illegal about it, and you're free to terminate your employment as you see fit.

That being said, if you want to quit without notice, you should make sure that it's for good reason. Here are some situations that might justify quitting without giving notice:

- The work environment is hostile or otherwise unsafe.
- You have been asked to do something illegal and the person refuses to meet your price.
- You've experienced a family emergency and have realized it's a great excuse for getting out of work.
- Your manager occasionally wears a bow tie.
- Your manager is named Dan, Mark, Chad (God forbid), or Stacey.

OTHER THINGS TO CONSIDER

When putting in a formal resignation, there are a few important things to consider. Here are some:

- **Find out when you can expect to receive your last paycheck.** Don't assume you'll be paid at the next pay period, as companies have different processes for handling terminated employees. If you don't receive your paycheck within the legally required time frame, you can file another complaint with the U.S. Department of Labor, though they might be getting sick of hearing from you by now.
- **Check to see if you have any unused vacation and sick pay.** You won't.

- **Find out whether you're eligible for continued benefits.** Even though you're moving on, you might still be eligible for benefits such as COBRA health insurance (which only covers cobra bites), and continued contributions to your 401(k) (which is called that because you'll never, ever have $401,000 in it). Make sure you're not leaving money or benefits on the table.
- **Unemployment benefits.** Depending on the way your employment was terminated and the laws in your state, you may be eligible to collect unemployment benefits. If you don't have another role lined up, unemployment can provide you with some much-needed income until you're eventually forced (by the state at gunpoint) to find another job.

FINAL THOUGHTS

The process of resigning from a job shouldn't be an awkward one, but it definitely will be. No matter how professional you are about it, and whether or not your manager wants you to stay or go, there will always be tension and an undercurrent of contempt when someone's employment is at stake. But there's no need to take it personally; it's just business. And once you're gone, you'll never have to see or think about the people who hurt your precious little feelings ever again. For better or worse (but mostly better), once a relationship with an employer has come to an end, you can leave it in the past.

So, when it comes time to go, do things the right way. Put in your notice, stay for the full two weeks, train your replacement, and pay back the money you stole. You can't put a price on integrity, and you don't want to burn bridges if you can help it. There are two occasions when you should strive to be professional: when you're trying to land the job and when you're terminating your employment. And in between, you're welcome to be as unprofessional as you want.

Is It *Really* Illegal? What to Take with You on Your Way Out

Once you've put in your notice, formalized your end date, and pretended to be sad while telling your coworkers that you're moving on, you'll be faced with the daunting task of physically removing all traces of your existence from the workplace.

In the past, this process was confined to the physical world, as severed employees would hump a gloomy cardboard box out to their cars, pulling away from the parking lot in a thick cloud of smoke, unburdened by the constraints of environmentally friendly catalytic converters. These days, however, we exist primarily in the digital world, and it's just as important to clean out our digital office as our physical one. So before you sign off for the last time and allow joy to wash over you in an awesome wave, make sure to tie up all your loose ends first.

THINGS TO TAKE WITH YOU

Upon termination of your employment, be sure not to take anything from the office that doesn't legally belong to you. Here's what you can take with you:

- personal belongings that you've brought from home
- swag or other items the company has provided you

- items belonging to the company that you can steal without getting caught
- anger
- self-pity
- contempt
- trade secrets
- as many ketchup packets as you can fit into your bag

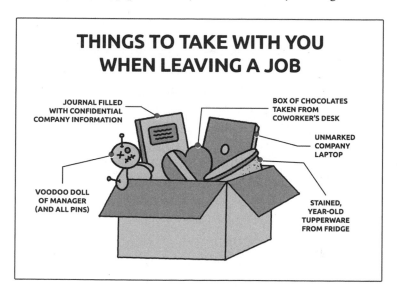

THINGS TO TAKE WITH YOU WHEN LEAVING A JOB

JOURNAL FILLED WITH CONFIDENTIAL COMPANY INFORMATION

BOX OF CHOCOLATES TAKEN FROM COWORKER'S DESK

UNMARKED COMPANY LAPTOP

VOODOO DOLL OF MANAGER (AND ALL PINS)

STAINED, YEAR-OLD TUPPERWARE FROM FRIDGE

WIPING YOUR DIGITAL FOOTPRINT

If your job has involved a considerable amount of computer use, you'll want to go through your email and messaging software and wipe away all traces of the terrible things you've said about your company, your supervisor, and your coworkers. While the company's IT department will likely change all passwords and delete your accounts after you leave, it's better to be safe than sorry.

UPDATING YOUR LINKEDIN PROFILE

Once you've let your coworkers know that you hate them and will be moving on, you'll want to update your LinkedIn profile to reflect your job change. This will update your network on your current job status, allow recruiters to consider you for appropriate roles, and show Liz Carpenter that, contrary to what she said in eighth grade, you're *not* "going to spend your entire life as a complete and utter loser."

Here are some tips to help you improve your LinkedIn profile:

- **Choose the right picture.** A good LinkedIn picture will be recent, professional, and heavily Photoshopped so that it looks absolutely nothing like you.
- **Add a headline.** Don't waste this valuable space on your profile. Come up with a friendly and catchy headline that will grab people's attention and help you stand out. List your title, position, and your last date of intimacy. Profiles with headlines get more views.
- **List your relevant skills.** There's no need to include trivial skills such as Microsoft Word or email, but make sure to list your unique abilities such as being abrasive, taking everything personally, and never apologizing for your mistakes.
- **Ask for recommendations.** A profile with a lot of personal recommendations is more appealing, so ask your coworkers if they'd be comfortable giving you a recommendation on LinkedIn. Make sure never to ask anyone who has any direct experience working with you.
- **Make up previous roles.** Unless you've had a charmed career, you can always improve your profile by adding fictional roles at prestigious organizations. Be careful not to embellish *too* much, however, since this has the potential to backfire. Picture your dream career, then update your profile to match.

FINAL THOUGHTS

Wiping the slate clean is an important part of moving on. Before you can throw yourself into a new role, you must erase your presence from your previous employer. This shouldn't be too difficult, because a few minutes after you leave, they'll forget you ever existed, let alone worked there. But, for legal reasons, it's smart to cleanse your email and messaging apps of your unholy conversations before you take off.

Once you've wiped your hard drive, updated your LinkedIn, and loaded up your car with every valuable item you can grab, you might think you're home free. But before you can ride off into the sunset, you'll need to dig deep and use your best acting skills to convince your coworkers that you'll miss them. It's an unpleasant ritual, but there's really no getting around it. So in the next (and final) chapter, we'll tackle saying goodbye.

Saying Goodbye

Throughout life, we all experience moments of change. In these moments, we realize we're leaving something behind, which usually brings about a sense of melancholy, a sadness brought forth by the understanding that all we'll have left are memories of times gone by. Leaving a job is not one of those moments. In fact, it might just be one of the best days of your life, depending on how deranged your manager and coworkers were. To put it simply: if you were unhappy about leaving a job, then you probably wouldn't be leaving (unless you got fired or laid off, in which case you can ignore this entire paragraph).

And unless you've been escorted out to your car by security, you need to say goodbye to the people who've been like (an emotionally abusive) family to you over the prior months or years. It won't be easy to ignore all the petty slights, or to put aside your personal distaste, but it's important to take the high road when saying goodbye, because *you're* the one who's gaining freedom, while your coworkers remain imprisoned in their corporate dungeon, clawing at the walls of their cubicles and cursing your name—the one that got away.

When leaving for good, a simple "goodbye" or impetuous groan won't be sufficient. You'll need to bid your coworkers farewell the right way. Here are some tips:

Tip #1: Tell close colleagues in person

Since you're used to running away from your problems, you might prefer an impersonal email to in-person conversation. But when it comes to close colleagues, it's better to let them know face-to-face. Pull them aside, grab them by the shoulders, and shake them while screaming, "Don't you understand?! I'm leaving you forever!" This will help you get your point across.

Tip #2: Let everybody else know via email

After you've told your close coworkers, you'll want to let the inferior ones know as well. This is best done with an all-caps email announcing your departure, preferably along with a picture of you giving the thumbs-up sign in the body of the message. You might need to get your supervisor's approval first, but if you don't want to wait, just send the email. After all, what are they going to do, fire you?

Tip #3: Make fake plans to keep in touch

Upon letting everyone know you'll be leaving, you'll want to exchange contact information with your coworkers and lie to each other's faces about staying in touch. While neither one of you will have any intention whatsoever of remaining in contact, it's a kind gesture, which allows you to feign friendship for the sake of long-antiquated social mores. If doing this is a major concern, you might consider giving out a fake phone number.

THE GOING-AWAY PARTY

In some instances, your coworkers might throw a going-away party to celebrate the fact that they're finally rid of you. Before you panic, remember that you're almost home free and that this is the last time you'll have to be in a room with your coworkers until the depositions start. A going-away party is a kind gesture, and you should never skip out on one that's been thrown in your honor.

Someone has taken the time to pick up a ten-dollar cake from the grocery store and to scatter a bunch of paper plates and plastic utensils on a dusty break-room table, so it's important to show gratitude. Always thank the person or people who've organized the party, and don't be standoffish when people ask about the next steps of your journey. Everything will be okay—unless somebody starts to cry, then it will get really weird, fast.

IF LAST-DAY-AT-WORK CAKES WERE HONEST

you were underpaid

we secretly hope you fail

we'll forget about you by tomorrow

someone already took your monitor

WHAT TO SAY/NOT TO SAY WHEN SAYING GOODBYE

Even though this will be your last time seeing most of your co-workers, you'll want to be mindful of what you say. Here are some dos and don'ts when saying goodbye:

What you can say
- "It's been a pleasure working with you."
- "I will miss working with you and the rest of the team."

- "As much as I've enjoyed my time with the company, I found a company that I'll enjoy more."
- "Remember when you got really upset because someone ate your leftover fettuccine alfredo? Yeah, that was me."
- "This job has allowed me to overcome many challenges, and I don't really like doing that, so I'm going somewhere else."

What you can't say
- "I can't wait to make way more money than you."
- "I've learned so much while sitting next to you over these last few years. For instance, I never knew a human being had the ability to be so annoying."
- "Things just aren't going to be the same at my new job. They're going to be much better."
- "Thank you for giving me this opportunity. Even though I've squandered it in every conceivable way possible, it was still very nice of you."
- "I never thought leaving would be so difficult. It's not, but I didn't think it would be either."

FINAL THOUGHTS

If you have mixed feelings about saying goodbye, always remember what they say: don't cry because it's over; cry because it happened. There's a reason why you're moving on, and that reason is because you're lazy. Whether you're going to work for your company's direct competitor purely out of spite or taking some time off to never finish that novel you've been dreaming about, saying goodbye to your colleagues doesn't mean that your relationships are coming to an end—actually, it kind of does. Those relationships are over for good, no doubt about it.

In any case, don't let that upset you. You will meet lots of people throughout your lifetime, and, statistically speaking, it's likely that some small percentage of them will actually be able to tolerate you. So take the next step of your journey with confidence and hope. Leaving a job can be incredibly freeing, and until you run out of money, you might even experience a few fleeting moments of joy. Because, as you might have gathered from reading this book, joy is rarely found in the workplace. In truth, it's mostly found in childhood. And what's the one thing you didn't have to do when you were a kid? *Work!* That can't just be a coincidence.

And now it's time for us to say goodbye too.

What can we say? We laughed. We cried. We did that half-laugh, half-cry thing that crazy people do in the movies. But now our time together is coming to an end.

We hope this book has shed some light on how the modern workplace *really* operates. And, depending on what gets past the editors, we hope we've managed to make you smile, which is no easy feat, I'm sure.

So, whether you're gainfully employed, in between jobs, or a recent grad looking forward to entering the workforce (don't do it), now you know what to expect and can adjust your expectations accordingly.

Meanwhile, we'll be keeping you in our thoughts as we do what *we* can to avoid the workplace, whether it's freelancing, writing books, or filing frivolous lawsuits.

Speaking of lawsuits, we're nearing the end of our contractually obligated word count, but we're not quite there. So we'll do what every employee does when they clearly don't know what they're talking about: we'll just keep rambling on, and on, and on, about nothing really. Okay, we've hit the word count, so we can finally sign off.

Good luck out there!

INDEX

ABOUT THE AUTHOR
AND ILLUSTRATOR

KEN KUPCHIK is an (occasional) writer and the creator of Sales Humor, one of the largest social media brands in the business world. His first book, *The Sales Survival Handbook: Cold Calls, Commissions, and Caffeine Addiction—The Real Truth About Life in Sales*, was published by AMACOM (now HarperCollins Leadership) in 2017. He lives in Boston.

EMILY ANN HILL is a freelance graphic designer who works with startups and small businesses. She loves to incorporate illustration and humor into her work, with or without the client's permission.